C SCIENCE HYMNAL

WORDS ONLY

With Seven Hymns Written by

THE REVEREND MARY BAKER EDDY

Discoverer and Founder of Christian Science

Marca Registrada

THE CHRISTIAN SCIENCE PUBLISHING SOCIETY
BOSTON, MASSACHUSETTS U.S.A.

The Church Dome and Tower Medallion
is a trademark of
The Christian Science Board of Directors.
Registered in the U.S. Patent and Trademark Office and in other countries.

The design of the colophon is a trademark of
The Christian Science Publishing Society

Published and Distributed by
The Christian Science Publishing Society
Boston, Massachusetts, United States of America

Study Edition Paperback ISBN: 978-0-87510-214-6
Study Edition Vivella® Sapphire Blue ISBN: 978-0-87510-409-6
Study Edition Vivella® Ruby Red ISBN: 978-0-87510-410-2
"Vivella®" is registered by Synt3 SpA, and is a non-leather,
entirely man-made material manufactured in Italy.

For information about reusing material from this work, please write:
Permissions
The Mary Baker Eddy Collection
One Norway Street, Boston, Massachusetts 02115
Email: permissions@marybakereddycollection.org

Printed in the United States of America
2007

Preface

For ages psalms and hymns have been used by Christian people to express their hopes and aspirations. Mary Baker Eddy, the Discoverer and Founder of Christian Science, was an appreciator of music and knew it could have a religious character. The love and truth expressed through the hymns in the *Christian Science Hymnal* have helped and comforted many, and will continue to do so in increased measure.

With the exception of the *Communion Doxology*, No. 1, the hymns are arranged alphabetically according to their first lines. Some were well-established standards when this volume was first published; others were selected because of association with the early history of the Christian Science movement. The hymns, "I need Thee every hour," "I'm a pilgrim, and I'm a stranger;" and *Eternity* were originally included in the *Hymnal* in accordance with Mrs. Eddy's wish.

You will find slight changes in the poems to make word accent conform to music accent. Other changes have been made in order to bring the thought of the poem into harmony with the teachings of Christian Science, but as far as possible, original wording of hymns has been preserved. An asterisk after the author's name indicates slight changes.

Grateful acknowledgment is due to the many contributors to the *Hymnal* and to authors and publishers who granted the use of copyrighted material and permitted such revision as would promote the unity and usefulness of the collection. When requested, copyright permissions have been acknowledged on the relevant pages. In many cases, however, where no specific copyright acknowledgments are shown, the hymns are nevertheless subject to copyright protection. Inquiries regarding the copyrights and permission to use hymns from the *Hymnal* should be directed to the Christian Science Board of Directors. The Publishers will welcome any report of omission of proper copyright acknowledgment and will gladly make correction in subsequent editions.

Woven throughout the structure of this *Hymnal*, with its songs of praise and gratitude to God, is the thought contained in the "Daily Prayer" of Christian Scientists, "and may Thy Word enrich the affections of all mankind, and govern them!" (*Church Manual* by Mary Baker Eddy, p. 41).

THE CHRISTIAN SCIENCE BOARD OF DIRECTORS

WORDS ONLY HYMNAL

ERRATA SHEET

Please make note of the following corrections:

Hymn 10
Third verse, fourth line - replace "him" with "Him"
("In Him we all are living.")

Hymn 66
Second verse, third line - replace "love" with "Love"
("Safe in Thy Love, we live...")

Hymn 82
First verse, first line - add the word "His"
("God is working His purpose out...")

Hymn 175
First verse, last line - add a period at the end
("We may know Thee and be free.")

Hymn 350
First verse, fifth line - replace "love" with "Love"
("Precious is the Love that healed us,")

Hymn 421
Second verse, third line - replace "love" with "Love"
("Safe in Thy Love, we live...")

EDB0705005

CHRISTIAN SCIENCE HYMNAL

WORDS ONLY

Be Thou, O God, exalted high;
And as Thy glory fills the sky,
So let it be on earth displayed,
Till Thou art here and now obeyed.

A glorious day is dawning,
And o'er the waking earth
The heralds of the morning
Are springing into birth.
In dark and hidden places
There shines the blessed light;
The beam of Truth displaces
The darkness of the night.

The advocates of error
Foresee the glorious morn,
And hear in shrinking terror,
The watchword of reform:
It rings from hill and valley,
It breaks oppression's chain.
A thousand freemen rally,
And swell the mighty strain.

The watchword has been spoken,
The light has broken forth,
Far shines the blessed token
Upon the startled earth.
To hearts and homes benighted
The blessed Truth is given,
And peace and love, united,
Point upward unto heaven.

A grateful heart a garden is,
Where there is always room
For every lovely, Godlike grace
To come to perfect bloom.

A grateful heart a fortress is,
A staunch and rugged tower,
Where God's omnipotence, revealed,
Girds man with mighty power.

A grateful heart a temple is,
A shrine so pure and white,
Where angels of His presence keep
Calm watch by day or night.

Grant then, dear Father-Mother, God,
Whatever else befall,
This largess of a grateful heart
That loves and blesses all.

A holy air is breathing round,
A fragrance from above:
Be every thought from sense unbound,
Be every action love.

O God, unite us heart to heart,
In sympathy divine,
That we be never drawn apart,
To love not Thee nor Thine;

But by the life of Jesus taught,
And all his gracious word,
Be nearer to each other brought,
And nearer Thee, O Lord.

A voice from heaven we have heard,
The call to rise from earth;
Put armor on, the sword now gird,
And for the fight go forth.
The foe in ambush claims our prize,
Then heed high heaven's call.
Obey the voice of Truth, arise,
And let not fear enthrall.

The cause requires unswerving might:
With God alone agree.
Then have no other aim than right;
End bondage, O be free.
Depart from sin, awake to love:
Your mission is to heal.
Then all of Truth you must approve,
And only know the real.

William H. Burleigh
Adapted

Abide not in the realm of dreams,
O man, however fair it seems;
But with clear eye the present scan,
And hear the call of God and man.

Think not in sleep to fold thy hands,
Forgetful of thy Lord's commands:
From duty's claims no life is free,
Behold, today hath need of thee.

The present hour allots thy task,
For present strength and patience ask;
And trust His love whose sure supply
Meets all thy need abundantly.

Bertha H. Woods
Based on hymn by H. F. Lyte

7

Abide with me; fast breaks the morning light;
Our daystar rises, banishing all night;
Thou art our strength, O Truth that maketh free,
We would unfailingly abide in Thee.

I know no fear, with Thee at hand to bless,
Sin hath no power and life no wretchedness;
Health, hope and love in all around I see
For those who trustingly abide in Thee.

I know Thy presence every passing hour,
I know Thy peace, for Thou alone art power;
O Love divine, abiding constantly,
I need not plead, Thou dost abide with me.

Abide with me; fast falls the eventide;
The darkness deepens; Lord, with me abide.
When other helpers fail, and comforts flee,
Help of the helpless, O abide with me.

I need Thy presence every passing hour;
What but Thy grace can foil the tempter's power?
Who like Thyself my guide and stay can be?
Through cloud and sunshine, O abide with me.

I fear no foe, with Thee at hand to bless;
Ills have no weight, and tears no bitterness;
Where is death's sting? where, grave, thy victory?
I triumph still, if Thou abide with me.

All glory be to God most high,
And on the earth be peace,
The angels sang, in days of yore,
The song that ne'er shall cease,
Till all the world knows peace.

God's angels ever come and go,
All winged with light and love;
They bring us blessings from on high,
They lift our thoughts above,
They whisper God is Love.

O longing hearts that wait on God
Through all the world so wide;
He knows the angels that you need,
And sends them to your side,
To comfort, guard and guide.

O wake and hear the angel-song
That bids all discord cease,
From pain and sorrow, doubt and fear,
It brings us sweet release;
And so our hearts find peace.

FREDERIC W. ROOT
Based on hymn by Martin Luther

All power is given unto our Lord,
On Him we place reliance;
With truth from out His sacred word
We bid our foes defiance.
With Him we shall prevail,
Whatever may assail;
He is our shield and tower,
Almighty is His power;
His kingdom is forever.

Rejoice, ye people, praise His name,
His care doth e'er surround us.
His love to error's thralldom came,
And from its chains unbound us.
Our Lord is God alone,
No other power we own;
No other voice we heed,
No other help we need;
His kingdom is forever.

O then give thanks to God on high,
Who life to all is giving;
The hosts of death before Him fly,
In him we all are living.
Then let us know no fear,
Our King is ever near;
Our stay and fortress strong,
Our strength, our hope, our song;
His kingdom is forever.

Angels at the Saviour's birth
Woke with music all the earth,
Shepherds in the eastern sky
Saw a pale star passing by,
Guiding them at break of day
Where the babe in meekness lay,
Born the gracious news to tell,
God with us, Immanuel.

Star of being, still thy light
Shines before us in the night,
By those radiant beams we find
Christ, the Truth, for all mankind,
Still the tidings angels bring
With their joyful caroling,
Telling that the dawn has come,
God and man fore'er at one.

12
—
13

VIOLET HAY

Arise ye people, take your stand,
Cast out your idols from the land,
Above all doctrine, form or creed
Is found the Truth that meets your need.
Christ's promise stands: they that believe
His works shall do, his power receive.

Go forward then, and as ye preach
So let your works confirm your speech,
And prove to all with following sign
The Word of God is power divine.
In love and healing ministry
Show forth the Truth that makes men free.

O Father-Mother God, whose plan
Hath given dominion unto man,
In Thine own image we may see
Man pure and upright, whole and free.
And ever through our work shall shine
That light whose glory, Lord, is Thine.

Arise, arise and shine,
On thee hath dawned the day;
God is thy sun, and Christ thy light,
Be thou a steadfast ray.

Sing praise, O waking heart,
For all thy God hath wrought;
For Truth's clear light on thee hath shone,
And purified thy thought.

No more shall sin and wrong
Obscure the light divine,
For God hath given thee His Son,
And lo, all things are thine.

Arise, arise and shine,
Uplift thee from the sod,
And let thy living light show forth
Man's unity with God.

15

Based on the Danish of
BERNHARD S. INGEMANN

As gold by fire is tested,
Its purity shown forth,
So cleansing fires of Truth may prove
To man his native worth.

And as a mirror shows us
A likeness clear and bright,
So God forever sees His child
Revealed in radiant light.

’Twas thus the loving Master
Saw man’s perfection shine,
Beheld God’s child forever pure
In radiance all divine.

As sings the mountain stream,
Past rock and verdure wild,
So let me sing my way to Thee,
Thy pure and happy child.

O boundless source of might,
My praise must e'er increase,
For Love is Life eternally,
Whose blessings never cease.

I sing my way today,
My heart is joyous, free,
For what is Thine is ever mine,
I find myself in Thee.

17

EDMUND BEALE SARGANT*
By permission of the author

Be firm, ye sentinels of Truth,
God's day of rest is near;
All scowling shapes of darkness flee;
The morning star shines clear.

Your constant challenge, Who goes there?
As idle words must cease.
How can the prince of this world now
Delay the Prince of Peace?

With healing in his wings he comes,
God's messenger of love,
'Tis yours to sound the trumpet call,
His Science yours to prove.

Be firm and be faithful; desert not the right;
The brave become bolder the darker the night.
Then up and be doing, though cowards may fail;
Thy duty pursuing, dare all and prevail.

If scorn be thy portion, if hatred and loss,
If stripes or a prison, remember the cross.
God watches above thee, and He will requite;
Forsake those that love thee, but never the right.

19

Based on the Danish of
HANS A. BRORSON

Behold, they stand in robes of white
Who out of tribulation came,
With songs of joy upon their heads,
They praise His holy name.
O these are they whose hearts are pure,
And free from sin or any stain,
They stand before the throne of light,
Their joy shall never wane.

They worship Him in spirit new,
God's messengers of Love and Life,
They do His will, they speak His Word,
That stills all pain and strife.
They show an ever clearer light,
Like stars they shall forever shine;
They witness truly to His Word,
And God saith, These are Mine.

Kate L. Colby
Adapted

Be true and list the voice within,
Be true unto thy high ideal,
Thy perfect self, that knows no sin,
That self that is the only real.

God is the only perfect One:
My perfect self is one with Him;
So man is seen as God's own son,
When Truth dispels the shadows dim.

True to our God whose name is Love,
We shall fulfill our Father's plan;
For true means true to God above,
To self, and to our fellow man.

Beloved, let us love: for Love is God;
In God alone hath love its true abode.

Beloved, let us love: for they who love,
They only, are His sons, born from above.

Beloved, let us love: for love is light,
And he who loveth not dwelleth in night.

Beloved, let us love: for only thus
Shall we behold that God who loveth us.

Blest Christmas morn, though murky clouds
Pursue thy way,
Thy light was born where storm enshrouds
Nor dawn nor day!

Dear Christ, forever here and near,
No cradle song,
No natal hour and mother's tear,
To thee belong.

Thou God-idea, Life-encrowned,
The Bethlehem babe—
Beloved, replete, by flesh embound—
Was but thy shade!

Thou gentle beam of living Love,
And deathless Life!
Truth infinite,—so far above
All mortal strife,

Or cruel creed, or earth-born taint:
Fill us today
With all thou art—be thou our saint,
Our stay, alway.

Breaking through the clouds of darkness,
Black with error, doubt, and fear;
Lighting up each somber shadow,
With a radiance soft and clear;
Filling every heart with gladness,
That its holy power feels,
Comes the Christian Science gospel,
Sin it kills and grief it heals.

Christlike in its benedictions,
Godlike in its strength sublime;
Conquering every subtle error,
With a meekness all divine,
It has gone across the ocean,
It is known in every land,
And our sisters and our brothers
Are united in one band.

Brood o'er us with Thy shelt'ring wing,
'Neath which our spirits blend
Like brother birds, that soar and sing,
And on the same branch bend.
The arrow that doth wound the dove
Darts not from those who watch and love.

If thou the bending reed wouldst break
By thought or word unkind,
Pray that his spirit you partake,
Who loved and healed mankind:
Seek holy thoughts and heavenly strain,
That make men one in love remain.

Learn, too, that wisdom's rod is given
For faith to kiss, and know;
That greetings glorious from high heaven,
Whence joys supernal flow,
Come from that Love, divinely near,
Which chastens pride and earth-born fear,

Through God, who gave that word of might
Which swelled creation's lay:
"Let there be light, and there was light."
What chased the clouds away?
'Twas Love whose finger traced aloud
A bow of promise on the cloud.

— *continued on next page* —

Thou to whose power our hope we give,
Free us from human strife.
Fed by Thy love divine we live,
For Love alone is Life;
And life most sweet, as heart to heart
Speaks kindly when we meet and part.

Call the Lord thy sure salvation,
Rest beneath th' Almighty's shade;
In His secret habitation
Dwell, nor ever be dismayed.

He shall charge His angel legions
Watch and ward o'er thee to keep,
Though thou walk through hostile regions,
Though in desert wilds thou sleep.

There no tumult can alarm thee,
Thou shalt dread no hidden snare;
Guile nor violence shall harm thee
In eternal safeguard there.

Christ comes again with holy power,
To lift our blinded eyes to see;
The sick are healed, the sinner blest,
As on that eve in Galilee.

Once more the lonely heart is fed.
Who dwells with Love hath perfect ease,
Faith, hope, and joy are with us all;
Great are companions such as these.

The weak and thirsty are refreshed,
Again each empty cup is filled;
The tender Christ is here to bless,
And all the storms of earth are stilled.

In Truth there is no pain or death
Nor any shades of coming night;
The promise of our God still stands:
At eventide it shall be light.

Christ, whose glory fills the skies,
Christ, the true, the perfect Light,
Sun of righteousness, arise,
Triumph o'er the shades of night;
Dayspring from on high, be near,
Daystar, in my heart appear.

Dark and cheerless is the morn
Uncompanioned, Lord, by thee;
Joyless is the day's return,
Till thy mercy's beams I see;
Till they inward light impart,
Glad my eyes, and warm my heart.

Visit then this soul of mine,
Pierce the gloom of sin and grief;
Fill me, radiancy divine,
Scatter all my unbelief;
More and more thyself display,
Shining to the perfect day.

HORATIUS BONAR
Adapted

Church of the ever-living God,
The Father's gracious choice;
Amid the voices of this earth
How mighty is thy voice.

Thy words, amid the words of earth,
How noiseless and how pure;
Amid the hurrying crowds of time
Thy step how calm and sure.

Amid the restless eyes of earth
How steadfast is thine eye,
Fixed on the silent loveliness
That fills the morning sky.

Untiring praise we lift on high,
Unfaltering songs we sing,
Unending festival we keep
In presence of the King.

City of God, how broad and far
Outspread thy walls sublime;
The true thy chartered freemen are,
Of every age and clime.

One holy church, one army strong,
One steadfast high intent,
One working band, one harvest song,
One King omnipotent.

How gleam thy watch fires through the night,
With never fainting ray;
How rise thy towers, serene and bright,
To meet the dawning day.

In vain the surge's angry shock,
In vain the drifting sands;
Unharmed upon th' eternal Rock,
The heavenly city stands.

39

SIMON BROWNE
Adapted

Come, gracious Spirit, heavenly Love,
With light and comfort from above;
Be Thou our guardian, Thou our guide,
O'er every thought and step preside.

The light of Truth to us display,
That we may know and choose Thy way;
Plant holy joy in every heart,
That we from Thee may ne'er depart.

Lead us, O Christ, thou living Way,
Nor let us from thy precepts stray;
Lead us to God, our heavenly rest,
That we may be forever blest.

Come, ye disconsolate, where'er ye languish,
Here health and peace are found, Life, Truth,
and Love;
Here bring your wounded hearts, here tell
your anguish;
Earth has no sorrow but Love can remove.

Joy of the desolate, light of the straying,
Hope of the penitent, fadeless and pure;
Here speaks the Comforter, tenderly saying,
Earth has no sorrow that Love cannot cure.

Here see the Bread of Life, see waters flowing
Forth from the throne of God, pure from above;
Come to the feast of love, come, ever knowing,
Earth has no sorrow but Love can remove.

41

JANE BORTHWICK
Adapted

Come, labor on:
Who dares stand idle on the harvest plain?
While all around him waves the golden grain,
And to each servant does the Master say,
Go work today.

Come, labor on:
Claim the high calling that we all may share;
To all the world the joyful tidings bear;
Redeem the time: its hours too swiftly fly,
Harvest draws nigh.

Come, labor on:
Away with gloomy doubts and faithless fear.
No arm so weak but may do service here;
By means the simplest can our God fulfill
His righteous will.

Come, labor on:
The toil is pleasant, the reward is sure;
Blessed are they who to the end endure;
How full their joy, how sweet their rest shall be,
O Lord, with Thee.

Come, Thou all-transforming Spirit,
Bless the sower and the seed;
Let each heart Thy grace inherit;
Raise the weak, the hungry feed;
From the Gospel, from the Gospel
Now supply Thy people's need.

O, may all enjoy the blessing
Which Thy holy word doth give;
Let us all, Thy love possessing,
Joyfully Thy truth receive;
And forever, and forever
To Thy praise and glory live.

Come unto me, ye weary,
And I will give you rest.
O tender words of Jesus,
Which come to hearts oppressed.
They tell of benediction,
Of pardon, grace, and peace,
Of joy that hath no ending,
Of love which cannot cease.

Come unto me, ye wanderers,
And I will give you light.
O loving words of Jesus,
Which come to cheer the night.
Come, all ye heavy laden,
And I will give you life.
O peaceful words of Jesus,
Which come to end all strife.

44

Come to the land of peace;
From shadows come away;
Where all the sounds of weeping cease,
And storms no more have sway.

Fear hath no dwelling here;
But pure repose and love
Breathe through the bright, celestial air
The spirit of the dove.

In this divine abode,
Change leaves no saddening trace;
Come, trusting heart, come to thy God,
Thy holy resting place.

Dear God, how glorious is Thy name
Through all the earth and sea and sky.
The wondrous heavens, Thy handiwork,
The moon and stars hast Thou ordained.

Such tender beauty, Lord, from Thee
Is shed abroad o'er all the earth;
In bird, in sunbeam, light and flower
Thy grace and goodness may be seen.

For this Thy gift unspeakable,
The beauty of Love's holiness,
We lift our hearts in grateful song
And would be always praising Thee.

46
—
47

Day by day the manna fell:
O, to learn this lesson well.
Still by constant mercy fed,
Give me, Lord, my daily bread.

Day by day the promise reads,
Daily strength for daily needs:
Cast foreboding fears away;
Take the manna of today.

Lord, my times are in Thy hand:
All my sanguine hopes have planned,
To Thy wisdom I resign,
And would mold my will to Thine.

Thou my daily task shalt give;
Day by day to Thee I live;
So shall added years fulfill
Not my own, my Father's will.

EDMUND BEALE SARGANT
By permission of the author

Dear Father-Mother, Thou dost grant
All good and perfect gifts to me;
'Tis mine to raise this beacon here,
Obedience unto Thee.

He knows not death who Life obeys,
Nor errs at all when Truth he heeds;
While merged in Love, what hold has hate
Upon his thoughts or deeds?

Eternal Life and Truth and Love,
They who obey Thine every call,
Thy freemen are, and freely have
Dominion over all.

49
—
50

Dear Lord and Father of us all,
Forgive our foolish ways;
Reclothe us in our rightful mind;
In purer lives Thy service find,
In deeper reverence, praise.

In simple trust like theirs who heard,
Beside the Syrian sea,
The gracious calling of the Lord,
Let us, like them, without a word
Rise up and follow thee.

Breathe through the pulses of desire
Thy coolness and Thy balm;
Let sense be dumb, let flesh retire;
Speak through the earthquake, wind and fire,
O still small voice of calm.

Drop Thy still dews of quietness,
Till all our strivings cease;
Take from us now the strain and stress,
And let our ordered lives confess
The beauty of Thy peace.

Eternal Mind the Potter is,
And thought th' eternal clay:
The hand that fashions is divine,
His works pass not away.
Man is the noblest work of God,
His beauty, power and grace,
Immortal; perfect as his Mind
Reflected face to face.

God could not make imperfect man
His model infinite;
Unhallowed thought He could not plan,
Love's work and Love must fit.
Life, Truth and Love the pattern make,
Christ is the perfect heir;
The clouds of sense roll back, and show
The form divinely fair.

God's will is done; His kingdom come;
The Potter's work is plain.
The longing to be good and true
Has brought the light again.
And man does stand as God's own child,
The image of His love.
Let gladness ring from every tongue,
And heaven and earth approve.

Based on a hymn by
JOHN R. MACDUFF

Everlasting arms of Love
Are beneath, around, above;
God it is who bears us on,
His the arm we lean upon.

He our ever-present guide
Faithful is, whate'er betide;
Gladly then we journey on,
With His arm to lean upon.

From earth's fears and vain alarms
Safe in His encircling arms,
He will keep us all the way,
God, our refuge, strength and stay.

Faith grasps the blessing she desires,
Hope points the upward gaze;
And Love, celestial Love, inspires
The eloquence of praise.

But sweeter far the still small voice
Unheard by human ear,
When God has made the heart rejoice,
And dried the bitter tear.

No accents flow, no words ascend;
All utterance faileth there;
But God Himself doth comprehend
And answer silent prayer.

Father, hear the prayer we offer;
Not for ease that prayer shall be,
But for strength, that we may ever
Live our lives courageously.

Not forever in green pastures
Do we ask our way to be,
But the steep and rugged pathway
May we tread rejoicingly.

Not forever by still waters
Would we idly quiet stay,
But would smite the living fountains
From the rocks along our way.

RAY PALMER
From the Latin. Adapted

Father, Thou joy of loving hearts,
Thou Fount of life, Thou Light of men,
From all the best that earth imparts,
We turn unfilled to Thee again.

Ever our longings turn to Thee,
O Thou on whom our care we cast;
Rejoicing when Thy smile we see,
And blest when faith can hold Thee fast.

Thy truth unchanged hath ever stood;
Thou savest those that on Thee call;
To them that seek Thee Thou art good;
To them that find Thee, All in all.

Frederick L. Hosmer
Adapted

Father, to Thee we turn away from sorrow,
Thou art the fountain whence our healing flows;
Dark though the night, joy cometh with the
morrow;
Safely they rest who on Thy love repose.

Should fond hopes fail and skies seem dark before us,
Should the vain cares that vex our days increase,
Comes with its calm the thought that Thou art
o'er us;
Then we grow quiet, folded in Thy peace.

Naught shall affright us, on Thy goodness leaning;
Low in the heart faith singeth still her song;
Chastened and blessed we learn life's deeper
meaning,
Thus in our meekness Thou dost make us strong.

Father, we Thy loving children
Lift our hearts in joy today,
Knowing well that Thou wilt keep us
Ever in Thy blessed way.
Thou art Love and Thou art wisdom,
Thou art Life and Thou art All;
In Thy Spirit living, moving,
We shall neither faint nor fall.

Come we daily then, dear Father,
Open hearts and willing hands,
Eager ears, expectant, joyful,
Ready for Thy right commands.
We would hear no other voices,
We would heed no other call;
Thou alone art good and gracious,
Thou our Mind and Thou our All.

In Thy house securely dwelling,
Where Thy children live to bless,
Seeing only Thy creation,
We can share Thy happiness,
Share Thy joy and spend it freely.
Loyal hearts can feel no fear;
We Thy children know Thee, Father,
Love and Life forever near.

Fight the good fight with all thy might,
Christ is thy strength, and Christ thy right;
Lay hold on Life, and it shall be
Thy joy and crown eternally.

Run the straight race through God's good grace,
Lift up thine eyes, and seek His face;
Life with its way before us lies,
Christ is the path, and Christ the prize.

Faint not nor fear, His arms are near;
He changeth not, and thou art dear;
On Him rely and thou shalt see
That Christ is all in all to thee.

62

63

From all that dwell below the skies
Let the Creator's praise arise;
Let the Redeemer's name be sung
Through every land, by every tongue.

Eternal are Thy mercies, Lord;
Eternal truth attends Thy word;
Thy praise shall sound from shore to shore,
Till suns shall rise and set no more.

From sense to Soul my pathway lies before me,
From mist and shadow into Truth's clear day;
The dawn of all things real is breaking o'er me,
My heart is singing: I have found the way.

I reach Mind's open door, and at its portal
I know that where I stand is holy ground;
I feel the calm and joy of things immortal,
The loveliness of Love is all around.

The way leads upward and its goal draws nearer,
Thought soars enraptured, fetterless and free;
The vision infinite to me grows clearer,
I touch the fringes of eternity.

65

Frances R. Havergal
Adapted

From glory unto glory,
Be this our joyous song;
From glory unto glory,
'Tis Love that leads us on;
As wider yet and wider,
The rising splendors glow,
What wisdom is revealed to us,
What freedom we may know.

The fullness of His blessing
Encompasseth our way;
The fullness of His promise
Crowns every dawning day;
The fullness of His glory
Is shining from above,
While more and more we learn to know
The fullness of His love.

From glory unto glory,
What great things He hath done,
What wonders He hath shown us,
What triumphs Love hath won.
From glory unto glory,
From strength to strength we go,
While grace for grace abundantly
Doth from His fullness flow.

From these Thy children gathered in Thy name,
From hearts made whole, from lips redeemed
from woe,
Thy praise, O Father, shall forever flow.
Alleluia! Alleluia!

O perfect Life, in Thy completeness held,
None can beyond Thy omnipresence stray;
Safe in Thy love, we live and sing alway
Alleluia! Alleluia!

O perfect Mind, reveal Thy likeness true,
That higher selfhood which we all must prove,
Joy and dominion, love reflecting Love,
Alleluia! Alleluia!

Thou, Soul, inspiring—give us vision clear,
Break earth-bound fetters, sweep away the veil,
Show the new heaven and earth that shall prevail.
Alleluia! Alleluia!

67
—
68

Charlotte Elliott
Adapted

Gird thy heavenly armor on,
Wear it ever night and day;
Ambushed lies the evil one:
Watch and pray.

Hear the victors who o'ercame;
Still they mark each warrior's way;
All with warning voice exclaim,
Watch and pray.

Hear, above all, hear thy Lord;
Him thou lovest to obey;
Hide within thy heart His word,
Watch and pray.

Give me, O Lord, an understanding heart,
That I may learn to know myself in Thee,
To spurn the wrong and choose the better part
And thus from sinful bondage be set free.

Give me, O Lord, a meek and contrite heart,
That I may learn to quell all selfish pride,
Bowing before Thee, see Thee as Thou art
And 'neath Thy sheltering presence safely hide.

Give me, O Lord, a gentle, loving heart,
That I may learn to be more tender, kind,
And with Thy healing touch, each wound and smart
With Christly bands of Love and Truth to bind.

God giveth light to all
Who ask with prayer sincere;
He doth not fail to hear that call;
His Truth is ever near.

Plain shall His guidance be,
If thou but seek the right;
Clearly thy pathway thou shalt see,
A line of purest light.

God is thy light and health;
No death nor darkness there;
Turn but to Him, accept His wealth,
And all His glory share.

Glorious things of thee are spoken,
Zion, city of our God;
He whose word cannot be broken,
Formed thee for His own abode:
On the Rock of Ages founded,
What can shake thy sure repose?
By salvation's walls surrounded
Thou mayst smile at all thy foes.

Round each habitation hovering,
See the cloud and fire appear
For a glory and a covering,
Showing that the Lord is near.
Thus deriving from their banner,
Light by night, and shade by day,
Safe they feed upon the manna,
Which He gives them when they pray.

See, the streams of living waters,
Springing from eternal Love,
Well supply thy sons and daughters,
And all fear of want remove.
Who can faint, while such a river
Ever shall their thirst assuage,
Grace, which like the Lord, the giver,
Never fails from age to age?

CHARLES WESLEY AND JOHN TAYLOR
Adapted

Glory be to God on high,
God whose glory fills the sky;
Peace on earth to man is given,
Man, the well-beloved of heaven.
Gracious Father, in Thy love,
Send Thy blessings from above;
Let Thy light, Thy truth, Thy peace
Bid all strife and tumult cease.

Mark the wonders of His hand:
Power no empire can withstand;
Wisdom, angels' glorious theme;
Goodness one eternal stream.
All ye people, raise the song,
Endless thanks to God belong;
Hearts o'erflowing with His praise
Join the hymns your voices raise.

Based on the Dutch of
ABRAHAM RUTGERS

73

Glory, honor, praise and pure oblations
Unto God the Lord belong;
Come into His presence with thanksgiving,
Come before Him with a song.
In His hand is all the power of nations,
Sing to Him, ye joyous congregations,
Psalms of gratitude and praise
Unto God the Father raise.

God is Mind and holy thought is sending;
Man, His image, hears His voice.
Every heart may understand His message,
In His kindness may rejoice.
Lo, He speaks, all condemnation ending,
Every true desire with Love's will blending;
Losing self, in Him we find
Joy, health, hope, for all mankind.

Go forth and stand upon the mount,
For Truth is at thy side;
The very rocks may seem to break,
And earth to open wide;
Yet error's tempest and its fire
Before that still small voice retire.

Go, take the little open book
From out the angel's hand;
The word of Truth is there for all
To read and understand.
What though the seven thunders roll?
That still small voice shall make thee whole.

JAMES MONTGOMERY
Adapted

God comes, with succor speedy,
To those who suffer wrong;
To help the poor and needy,
And bid the weak be strong;
He comes to break oppression,
To set the captive free,
To take away transgression,
And rule in equity.

His blessings come as showers
Upon the thirsty earth;
And joy and hope, like flowers,
Spring in His path to birth.
Before Him on the mountains
Shall Peace, the herald, go;
From hill to vale the fountains
Of righteousness shall flow.

To Him shall prayer unceasing,
And daily vows, ascend;
His kingdom still increasing,
A kingdom without end.
The tide of time shall never
His covenant remove;
His name shall stand forever:
His changeless name of Love.

76

Johannes Heermann. *From the Swedish translation of Jakob Boëthius and Johan O. Wallin, Adapted.*

God is known in loving-kindness,
God, the true, eternal good;
Zion, ne'er will He forsake thee,
Trust His Father-Motherhood.
Can a mother leave her children?
Can unchanging Love forget?
Though all earthly friends betray thee,
Lo, His arm enfolds thee yet.

Every prayer to Him is answered,
Prayer confiding in His will;
Blessedness and joy are near thee,
Hear His gentle Peace, be still.
Hear His voice above the tempest:
I have not forsaken thee;
In My hand thy name is graven,
I will save both thine and thee.

God is my strong salvation;
What foe have I to fear?
In darkness and temptation,
My light, my help is near:
Though hosts encamp around me,
Firm in the fight I stand;
What terror can confound me,
With God at my right hand?

Place on the Lord reliance;
My heart, with courage wait;
His truth be thine affiance,
When faint and desolate:
His might thy heart shall strengthen,
His love thy joy increase;
Thy day shall mercy lengthen:
The Lord will give thee peace.

John Bowring*

God is Love; His mercy brightens
All the path in which we rove;
Bliss He wakes and woe He lightens;
God is wisdom, God is Love.

E'en the hour that darkest seemeth,
Will His changeless goodness prove;
Through the mist His brightness streameth;
God is wisdom, God is Love.

He with earthly cares entwineth
Hope and comfort from above;
Everywhere His glory shineth;
God is wisdom, God is Love.

God is our refuge and defense,
In trouble our unfailing aid;
Secure in His omnipotence,
What foe can make our heart afraid?

There is a river pure and bright,
Whose streams make glad the heavenly plains;
Where, in eternity of light,
The city of our God remains.

Built by the word of His command,
With His unclouded presence blest,
Firm as His throne the bulwarks stand;
There is our home, our hope, our rest.

81

THEODORE C. WILLIAMS
Adapted

God is with me, gently o'er me
Are His wings of mercy spread;
All His way made plain before me,
And His glory round me shed.
Safely onward
Shall my pilgrim feet be led.

God is with me, and His presence
Shall my perfect guidance be,
Till my heart that peace inherit
God alone can give to me.
His all-power
Helps and heals, and sets me free.

God is working purpose out
As year succeeds to year,
God is working His purpose out
And the time is drawing near;
Nearer and nearer draws the time,
The time that shall surely be,
When the earth shall be filled with
the glory of God
As the waters cover the sea.

What can we do to work God's work,
To prosper and increase
The brotherhood of all mankind,
The reign of the Prince of Peace?
What can we do to hasten the time,
The time that shall surely be,
When the earth shall be filled with
the glory of God
As the waters cover the sea?

March we forth in the strength of God
With the banner of Christ unfurled,
That the light of the glorious Gospel of truth
May shine throughout the world;
Fight we the fight with sorrow and sin,
To set their captives free,
That the earth may be filled with
the glory of God
As the waters cover the sea.

83

JAMES MONTGOMERY
Adapted

God made all His creatures free;
Life itself is liberty;
God ordained no other bands
Than united hearts and hands.

One in fellowship of Mind,
We our bliss and glory find
In that endless happy whole,
Where our God is Life and Soul.

So shall all our slavery cease,
All God's children dwell in peace,
And the newborn earth record
Love, and Love alone, is Lord.

Based on a hymn by
THEODOR V. OLDENBURG

God's eternal Word is spoken,
Piercing mists, around, above;
Of eternal might the token,
Emblem of eternal Love;
Out of darkness, world-enthralling,
Into Light, O hear it calling.

Word of God, O Word eternal,
May we hear thy living voice,
Learn the power of Love supernal,
Learn obedience,—and rejoice;
God's commands forever heeding,
Follow where His love is leading.

God of Truth, eternal good,
Lift our hearts to revelation,
That Thou mayst be understood,
Thou, the Rock of our salvation;
All Thy love we have for loving,
All Thy truth is ours for proving.

Open now our eyes to see,
As the clouds of sense are riven,
We behold reality,
Know the glory of Thy heaven;
So we seek Thy perfect healing
Through the Truth of Thy revealing.

All the way that we must go
We will take at Thy direction,
Where the floods of trouble flow
Find Thy perfect, calm reflection;
On the path that has no turning,
Patience, courage, meekness learning.

God's glory is a wondrous thing,
Most strange in all its ways,
And of all things on earth, least like
What men agree to praise.

O blest is he to whom is given
The instinct that can tell
That God is on the field, although
He seems invisible.

And blest is he who can divine
Where right doth really lie,
And dares to side with what seems wrong
To mortals' blindfold eye.

For right is right, since God is God;
And right the day must win;
To doubt would be disloyalty,
To falter would be sin.

88
—
89

THOMAS T. LYNCH*

Gracious Spirit, dwell with me:
I myself would gracious be,
And with words that help and heal
Would Thy life in mine reveal;
And with actions bold and meek
Christ's own gracious spirit speak.

Truthful Spirit, dwell with me:
I myself would truthful be,
And with wisdom kind and clear
Let Thy life in mine appear;
And with actions brotherly
Follow Christ's sincerity.

Mighty Spirit, dwell with me:
I myself would mighty be,
Mighty, that I may prevail
Where unaided man must fail;
Ever by triumphant hope
Pressing on and bearing up.

William Williams
From his hymn in Welsh, Adapted

Guide me, O Thou great Jehovah,
Pilgrim through this barren land:
I am Thine, and Thou art mighty,
Hold me with Thy powerful hand.
Bread of heaven! Bread of heaven!
Feed me now and evermore.

Open is the crystal fountain,
Whence the healing waters flow;
And the fiery cloudy pillar
Leads me all my journey through.
Strong Deliverer! Strong Deliverer!
Still Thou art my strength and shield.

Grace for today, O Love divine,
Thee to obey and love alone;
Losing the mortal will in Thine,
Find we a joy before unknown.

Grace for today, Thou Love divine,
Famishing hearts and hopes to feed;
Blot out all fear, let Thy light shine
With tender warmth on all our need.

Grace for today, Thou Love divine,
Patient of heart his way to trace
Whose pure affections Thee define
In tender love and perfect grace.

Thomas Cogswell Upham

Adapted

Happy the man who knows
His Master to obey;
Whose life of love and labor flows,
Where God points out the way.

Rising to every task,
Soon as the word is given,
He doth not wait nor question ask
When orders come from heaven.

God's will he makes his own,
And nothing can him stay;
His feet are shod for God alone,
And God alone obey.

Give us, O God, this mind,
Which waits but Thy command,
And doth its highest pleasure find
In Thy great work to stand.

Happy the man whose heart can rest,
Assured God's goodness ne'er will cease;
Each day, complete, with joy is blessed,
God keepeth him in perfect peace.

God keepeth him, and God is one,
One Life, forevermore the same,
One Truth unchanged while ages run;
Eternal Love His holiest name.

Dwelling in Love that cannot change,
From anxious fear man finds release;
No more his homeless longings range,
God keepeth him in perfect peace.

In perfect peace, with tumult stilled,
Enhavened where no storms arise,
There man can work what God hath willed;
The joy of perfect work his prize.

STEPHEN G. BULFINCH
Adapted

Hath not thy heart within thee burned
At evening's calm and holy hour,
As if its inmost depths discerned
The presence of a loftier power?

It was the voice of God that spake
In silence to thy silent heart,
And bade each worthier thought awake,
And every dream of earth depart.

O voice of God, forever near,
In low, sweet accents whispering peace,
Make us Thy harmonies to hear
Whose heavenly echoes never cease.

He leadeth me, O blessed thought,
O words with heavenly comfort fraught.
Whate'er I do, where'er I be,
Still 'tis God's hand that leadeth me.

REFRAIN
He leadeth me, He leadeth me,
By His own hand He leadeth me.
His faithful follower I would be,
For by His hand He leadeth me.

Sometimes mid scenes of deepest gloom,
Sometimes where Eden's bowers bloom,
By waters calm, o'er troubled sea,
Still 'tis His hand that leadeth me.

REFRAIN

He stood of old, the holy Christ,
Amid the suffering throng,
With whom his lightest touch sufficed
To make the weakest strong.
That healing gift God gives to them
Who use it in His name;
The power that filled the garment's hem
Is evermore the same.

So shalt thou be with power endued
Like him who went about
The Syrian hillsides doing good
And casting demons out.
The Great Physician liveth yet
Thy friend and guide to be;
The Healer by Gennesaret
Shall walk the rounds with thee.

THOMAS HASTINGS
Adapted

He that goeth forth with weeping,
Bearing still the precious seed,
Never tiring, never sleeping,
Soon shall see his toil succeed;
Showers of rain will fall from heaven,
Then the cheering sun will shine;
So shall plenteous fruit be given,
Through an influence all divine.

Sow thy seed, be never weary,
Let not fear thy thoughts employ;
Though the prospect seem most dreary,
Thou shalt reap the fruits of joy:
Lo, the scene of verdure brightening,
See the rising grain appear;
Look again, the fields are whitening,
Harvest time is surely here.

Ninety-first Psalm I

Adapted from Tate and Brady

He that hath God his guardian made,
Shall underneath th' Almighty's shade
Fearless and undisturbed abide;
Thus to myself of Him I'll say,
He is my fortress, shield and stay,
My God; in Him I will confide.

His tender love and watchful care
Shall free thee from the fowler's snare,
From every harm and pestilence.
He over thee His wings shall spread
To cover thy unguarded head.
His truth shall be thy strong defense.

He gives His angels charge o'er thee,
No evil therefore shalt thou see;
Thy refuge shall be God most high;
Dwelling within His secret place,
Thou shalt behold His power and grace,
See His salvation ever nigh.

Ninety-first Psalm II

Varied from Tate and Brady

He that hath God his guardian made
Shall dwell beneath th' Almighty's shade;
Thus of the Lord I now will say,
He is my fortress, shield and stay,
My God; in Him I will confide
And in His secret place abide.

His tender love and watchful care
Shall free thee from the fowler's snare.
He over thee His wings shall spread,
To cover thy unguarded head,
And from the noisome pestilence
His truth shall be thy strong defense.

He gives His angels charge o'er thee,
No evil therefore shalt thou see.
Dwelling within His secret place,
Thou shalt behold His power and grace;
Thy refuge shall be God most high,
See His salvation ever nigh.

He sent His Word, His holy Word,
And grieving hearts were healed;
Uplifted they beheld in light
Man's heritage revealed;
For this we bless Thee, Lord.

He sent His Word, His shining Word
Of Truth, forever one,
And sons of men rejoice to know
The dream of sorrow done;
For this we bless Thee, Lord.

He sent His Word, His faithful Word,
And hosts who toil in vain
Reject the falsehood ages taught
And rise to Life again;
For this we bless Thee, Lord.

102

103

Hear our prayer, O gracious Father,
Author of celestial good,
That Thy laws so pure and holy
May be better understood.

Armed with faith, may we press onward,
Knowing nothing but Thy will;
Conquering every storm of error
With the sweet words: Peace, be still.

Like the star of Bethlehem shining,
Love will guide us all the way,
From the depths of error's darkness
Into Truth's eternal day.

Help us, O Lord, to bear the cross,
The cross our Master bore;
To brave the senses' angry shock,
Our faith secure upon the rock
Of Christ, forevermore.

Grant us, O Love, the strength to drink
Thy cup on earth below,
The inspiration that it brings,
The hope serene that from it springs
To lighten every woe.

Give us, O Truth, Thou light of men,
Thy benediction rare,
That courage may sustain our way
Out of the darkness into day,
Thy day, celestial, fair.

Thus shall our Spirit, Mind divine,
Lead us to heaven's bowers:
The cross laid down; the victory won
O'er sense and self; revealed the Son;
The crown forever ours.

Help us to help each other, Lord,
Each other's cross to bear;
Let each his friendly aid afford,
And feel his brother's care.

Help us to build each other up,
Our little stock improve;
Increase our faith, confirm our hope,
And perfect us in love.

Up unto Thee, our living Head,
Let us in all things grow;
Till Thou hast made us free indeed,
And spotless here below.

Here, O my Lord, I'd see Thee face to face;
Here would I touch and handle things unseen;
Here grasp with firmer hand th' eternal grace,
And all my weariness upon Thee lean.

Here would I feed upon the bread of God;
Here drink anew the royal wine of heaven;
Here would I lay aside each earthly load,
Here taste afresh the calm of sin forgiven.

And as we rise, the symbols disappear;
The feast, though not the love, is past and gone;
The bread and wine remove, but Thou art here,
Nearer than ever, still my shield and sun.

Feast after feast thus comes and passes by;
Yet passing, points to the glad feast above,
Giving sweet foretaste of the festal joy,
The Lamb's great bridal feast of bliss and love.

Here, O God, Thy healing presence
Lifts our thoughts from self and sin,
Fills with light their hidden places,
When Thy love is welcomed in.
Here Thy tender sweet persuasions
Turn us home to heavenly ways,
While our hearts, unsealed, adoring,
Pour the fragrance of Thy praise.

Reverent lives unveil Thy beauty,
Faithful witness bear of Thee;
Binding up the brokenhearted,
We reflect Thy radiancy.
So may deeper consecration
Show Thee forth in healing's sign,
Till through joyful self-surrender
We in Love's pure likeness shine.

High in the heavens, eternal God,
Thy goodness in full glory shines;
Thy truth shall break through every cloud
That veils and darkens Thy designs.

Forever firm Thy justice stands,
As mountains their foundations keep:
How wise the wonders of Thy hands;
Thy judgments are a mighty deep.

Life, like a fountain rich and free,
Springs from the presence of my Lord;
And in Thy light we all shall see
The glories promised in Thy Word.

High to heaven let song be soaring,
Borne on faith's triumphant pinion;
Free from sin, our hearts adoring
Yield themselves to Love's dominion.

Sing, till all the world rejoices,
Sing! for fear no more enslaves us.
From th' accuser's mocking voices
Christ, our mighty Counsel, saves us.

Sing the Word, whose power supernal
Loveliness and joy unfoldeth;
Man who lives in Life eternal
Evermore the light beholdeth.

FROM THE ARMENIAN LITURGY
Translated by Leon Tourian, Adapted

Holiness becomes Thy house,
'Tis Thou who dost dwell in light;
Thou begirt with majesty,
Gird us with Truth,
And with Thy great might.

Send Thou forth Thy power and love,
In beauty of holiness;
We would here commune with Thee,
Eternal God,
Be Thou near to bless.

O supreme and perfect One,
O Lord, praise to Thee is due;
Clothe us in the grace of love,
Maintain Thy church
To Thy service true.

JOHN BURTON
Adapted

Holy Bible, book divine,
Precious treasure, thou art mine:
Mine to tell me whence I came;
Mine to tell me what I am;

Mine to chide me when I rove,
Mine to show a Saviour's love;
Mine thou art to guide and guard;
Mine to give a rich reward;

Mine to comfort in distress,
With a Saviour's tenderness;
Mine to show, by living faith,
Man can triumph over death.

JOHN M. NEALE
Adapted

Holy Father, Thou hast taught us
We should live to Thee alone;
Year by year, Thy hand hath brought us
On through dangers oft unknown.
When we wandered, Thou hast found us;
When we doubted, sent us light;
Still Thine arm has been around us,
All our paths were in Thy sight.

We would trust in Thy protecting,
Wholly rest upon Thine arm,
Follow wholly Thy directing,
Thou our only guard from harm.
Keep us from our own undoing,
Help us turn to Thee when tried,
Still our strength in Thee renewing,
Keep us ever at Thy side.

Holy, Holy, Holy, Lord God Almighty,
Early in the morning our song shall rise to Thee.
Holy, Holy, Holy, merciful and mighty,
Which wert, and art, and evermore shalt be.

Holy, Holy, Holy, darkness cannot hide Thee,
Though the eyes of sinful men Thy glory cannot see.
Thou alone art holy, there is none beside Thee,
Perfect in power, in love and purity.

Holy, Holy, Holy, Lord God Almighty,
All Thy works shall praise Thy name in earth,
and sky and sea;
Holy, Holy, Holy, merciful and mighty,
Which wert, and art, and evermore shalt be.

ANDREW REED AND SAMUEL LONGFELLOW
Adapted

118

Holy Spirit, Light divine,
Shine upon this heart of mine;
Kindle every high desire;
Cleanse my thought in Thy pure fire.

Holy Spirit, Peace divine,
Still this restless heart of mine;
Speak to calm the tossing sea,
Stayed in Thy tranquillity.

Holy Spirit, all divine,
Dwell within this heart of mine;
Bid my troubled thoughts be still;
With Thy peace my spirit fill.

119

PAUL GERHARDT
JOHN CHRISTIAN JACOBI, TR., *Adapted*

Holy Spirit, source of gladness,
Come with all Thy radiance bright;
Lift all burdens and all sadness;
O'er Thy children shed Thy light.

Let the Love that knows no measure,
Now in quickening showers descend;
Bring to us the richest treasure
Man can wish or God can send.

Send us Thine illumination;
Banish all our fears at length;
Rest upon this congregation,
Spirit of unfailing strength.

How beauteous on the mountains
The feet of him that brings,
Like streams from living fountains,
Good tidings of good things;
That publishes salvation;
From error gives release
To every tribe and nation:
God's reign of joy and peace.

Break forth in hymns of gladness,
O waste Jerusalem;
Let songs instead of sadness,
Thy jubilee proclaim;
The Lord, in strength victorious,
Upon thy foes has trod;
Behold, O earth, the glorious
Salvation of our God.

121
122

WILLIAM GOODE*

How blest are they whose hearts are pure;
From guile their thoughts are free,
To them shall God reveal Himself,
They shall His glory see.

They truly rest upon His word
In fullest light of love;
In this their trust, they ask no more
Than guidance from above.

They who in faith unmixed with doubt
Th' engrafted word receive,
Whom every sign of heavenly power
Persuades, and they believe,—

For them far greater things than these
Doth Christ the Lord prepare;
Whose bliss no human heart can reach,
No human voice declare.

"K" in Rippon's Selection, 1787
Adapted

How firm a foundation, ye saints of the Lord,
Is laid for your faith in His excellent Word.
What more can He say than to you He hath said,
To you who to God for your refuge have fled:

Fear not, I am with thee, O be not dismayed,
For I am thy God, I will still give thee aid;
I'll strengthen thee, help thee, and cause thee to stand,
Upheld by My gracious, omnipotent hand;

When through fiery trials thy pathway shall lie,
My grace, all sufficient, shall be thy supply;
The flame shall not hurt thee; I only design
Thy dross to consume and thy gold to refine.

Philip Doddridge
Adapted

How gentle God's commands,
How kind His precepts are;
Come, cast your burdens on the Lord,
And trust His constant care.

Beneath His watchful eye
His saints securely dwell;
That hand which bears creation up
Shall guard His children well.

His goodness stands approved,
Unchanged from day to day:
I drop my burden at His feet,
And bear a song away.

John Milton
Adapted

How lovely are Thy dwellings, Lord,
From noise and trouble free;
How beautiful the sweet accord
Of those who pray to Thee.

Lord God of Hosts, that reigns on high,
They are the truly blest
Who on Thee only will rely,
In Thee alone will rest.

For God the Lord, both sun and shield,
Gives grace and glory bright;
No good from him shall be withheld
Whose ways are just and right.

126
―
127

Joseph Swain
Adapted

How sweet, how heavenly is the sight,
When those who love the Lord
In one another's peace delight,
And so fulfill His word;

When, free from envy, scorn, and pride,
Our wishes all above,
Each can his brother's failings hide,
And show a brother's love.

Let love, in one delightful stream,
Through every bosom flow;
And union sweet, and dear esteem
In every action glow.

Love is the golden chain that binds
The hearts that faithful prove;
And he's an heir of heaven who finds
His bosom glow with love.

John Bowring
Adapted

How sweetly flowed the gospel sound
From lips of gentleness and grace,
When listening thousands gathered round
And joy and reverence filled the place.

From heaven he came, of heaven he spoke,
To heaven he led his followers' way.
Dark clouds of gloomy night he broke,
Unveiling Love's immortal day.

To wanderers from the Father's home,
To weary ones he offered rest;
So to his teachings all may come,
Obey them, love them, and be blest.

Psalm 36
From Danish Version

How wondrous is Thy mercy, Lord,
How faithful is Thy kindness.
Thou gav'st the treasure of Thy Word;
That Word dispels all blindness.
Thou holdest all things in Thy sight,
For in Thy presence is no night,
And in Thy light shall we see light.

Thy judgments are a mighty deep,
Thy wisdom past all seeking;
Thou watchest when we lie asleep,
We trust us to Thy keeping.
Thy love doth every blessing shower;
It rests alike on man and flower:
The whole creation owns Thy power.

131

132

I am the way, the truth, the life,
Our blessed Master said;
And whoso to the Father comes,
Must in my pathway tread:

A way that is not hedged with forms;
A truth, too large for creeds;
A life, indwelling, deep and broad,
That meets the heart's great needs.

To point that living way, to speak
The truth that makes men free,
To bring that quick'ning life from heaven,
Is highest ministry.

I cannot always trace the way
Where Thou, Almighty One, dost move;
But I can always, always say
That God is Love, that God is Love.

When mystery clouds my darkened path,
I conquer dread and doubts reprove;
In this my heart sweet comfort hath,
That God is Love, that God is Love.

Yes, God is Love: a thought like this
Can every gloomy thought remove,
And turn all tears, all woes, to bliss,
For God is Love, for God is Love.

I look to Thee in every need,
And never look in vain;
I feel Thy touch, eternal Love,
And all is well again:
The thought of Thee is mightier far
Than sin and pain and sorrow are.

Thy calmness bends serene above,
My restlessness to still;
Around me flows Thy quickening life
To nerve my faltering will:
Thy presence fills my solitude;
Thy providence turns all to good.

Embosomed deep in Thy dear love,
Held in Thy law, I stand:
Thy hand in all things I behold,
And all things in Thy hand.
Thou leadest me by unsought ways,
Thou turn’st my mourning into praise.

135

Carl J. P. Spitta
Richard Massie, Tr., *Adapted*

I know no life divided,
O Lord of life, from Thee;
In Thee is life provided
For all mankind and me:
I know no death, O Father,
Because I live in Thee;
Thy life it is that frees us
From death eternally.

I fear no tribulation,
Since, whatsoe'er it be,
It makes no separation
Between my Lord and me:
Since Thou, my God and Father,
Dost claim me as Thine own,
I richly shall inherit
All good, from Thee alone.

I love Thy way of freedom, Lord,
To serve Thee is my choice,
In Thy clear light of Truth I rise
And, listening for Thy voice,
I hear Thy promise old and new,
That bids all fear to cease:
My presence still shall go with thee
And I will give thee peace.

Though storm or discord cross my path
Thy power is still my stay,
Though human will and woe would check
My upward-soaring way;
All unafraid I wait, the while
Thy angels bring release,
For still Thy presence is with me,
And Thou dost give me peace.

I climb, with joy, the heights of Mind,
To soar o'er time and space;
I yet shall know as I am known
And see Thee face to face.
Till time and space and fear are naught
My quest shall never cease,
Thy presence ever goes with me
And Thou dost give me peace.

ANNIE S. HAWKS*

I need Thee every hour,
Most gracious Lord;
No tender voice like Thine
Can peace afford.

REFRAIN

I need Thee, O, I need Thee;
Every hour I need Thee;
O bless me now, my Saviour,
I come to Thee.

I need Thee every hour;
Stay Thou near by;
Temptations lose their power
When Thou art nigh.

REFRAIN

I need Thee every hour;
Teach me Thy will;
And Thy rich promise, Lord,
In me fulfill.

REFRAIN

Samuel Johnson
Adapted

I praise Thee, Lord, for blessings sent
To break the dream of human power;
For now, my shallow cistern spent,
I find Thy font and thirst no more.

I take Thy hand and fears grow still;
Behold Thy face and doubts remove;
Who would not yield his wavering will
To perfect Truth and boundless Love?

That Truth gives promise of a dawn
Beneath whose light I am to see,
When all these blinding veils are drawn,
Thy love has always guided me.

I walk with Love along the way,
And O, it is a holy day;
No more I suffer cruel fear,
I feel God's presence with me here;
The joy that none can take away
Is mine; I walk with Love today.

Who walks with Love along the way,
Shall talk with Love and Love obey;
God's healing truth is free to all,
Our Father answers every call;
'Tis He dispels the clouds of gray
That all may walk with Love today.

Come, walk with Love along the way,
Let childlike trust be yours today;
Uplift your thought, with courage go,
Give of your heart's rich overflow,
And peace shall crown your joy-filled day.
Come, walk with Love along the way.

John Keble
Adapted

140

If on our daily course, our mind
Be set to hallow all we find,
New treasures still, of countless price,
God will provide for sacrifice.

Old friends, old scenes, will lovelier be,
As more of heaven in each we see;
Some softening gleam of love and prayer
Shall dawn on every cross and care.

New mercies, each returning day,
Around us hover while we pray;
Old fears are past, old sins forgiven,
New thoughts of God reveal our heaven.

If the Lord build not the house
They that labor build in vain;
Father, may our corner stone
Stand foursquare, without a stain.

Make our planting timely, true,
Governed by a power benign;
Nourish by a heavenly dew
All the branches and the vine.

Fruitful shall our tillage be,
Known the work of perfect Mind,
Leaves be gathered from the tree
For the healing of mankind.

Cleansing men of fear and hate,
Lifting hope above the sod,
Truth will summon, soon or late,
All the earth to worship God.

Immortal Love, forever full,
Forever flowing free,
Forever shared, forever whole,
A never ebbing sea,—

Our outward lips confess the name
All other names above;
But love alone knows whence it came,
And comprehendeth Love.

Blow, winds of God, awake and blow
The mists of earth away.
Shine out, O light divine, and show
How wide and far we stray.

The letter fails, the systems fall,
And every symbol wanes:
The Spirit overbrooding all,
Eternal Love, remains.

143

THOMAS SCOTT
Adapted

Imposture shrinks from light,
And dreads the piercing eye;
But sacred truths the test invite,
They bid us search and try.

With understanding blest,
Created to be free,
Our faith, O God, on Thee we rest,
Obeying none but Thee.

The truth Thou dost impart
May we with firmness own,
Abhorring each evasive art,
And loving Thee alone.

H.
Adapted

In atmosphere of Love divine,
We live, and move, and breathe;
Though mortal eyes may see it not,
'Tis sense that would deceive.

The mortal sense we must destroy,
If we would bring to light
The wonders of eternal Mind,
Where sense is lost in sight.

For God, immortal Principle,
Is with us everywhere;
He holds us perfect in His love,
And we His image bear.

146
147

Violet Ker Seymer

In God I find a precious gift
That knows no fear, no feud,
That glows so still, serene and pure:
The gift of gratitude.

It brightens all the paths of earth,
Reflecting Truth and right,
For gratitude doth steadfastly
Abide in heavenly light.

With confidence it hails each task,
With courage undismayed,
For naught against Infinity
Can ever be arrayed.

In seamless gratitude I weave
A silent, healing prayer,
With shining threads of ceaseless joy;
For man is God's great heir.

In heavenly Love abiding,
No change my heart shall fear;
And safe is such confiding,
For nothing changes here.
The storm may roar without me,
My heart may low be laid;
But God is round about me,
And can I be dismayed?

Wherever He may guide me,
No want shall turn me back;
My Shepherd is beside me,
And nothing can I lack.
His wisdom ever waketh,
His sight is never dim;
He knows the way He taketh,
And I will walk with Him.

Green pastures are before me,
Which yet I have not seen;
Bright skies will soon be o'er me,
Where darkest clouds have been.
My hope I cannot measure,
My path in life is free;
My Father has my treasure,
And He will walk with me.

In Love divine all earth-born fear and sorrow
Fade as the dark when dawn pours forth her light;
And understanding prayer is fully answered,
When trustingly we turn to God aright.

And as on wings of faith we soar and worship,
Held by God's love above the shadows dim,
Hushed in the grandeur of a heart's awakening,
Unfolds a joy unknown till found in Him.

Then in this radiant light of adoration,
We know that man beloved is in God's care,
Not wrapt in fear nor bowed with tired labor,
But satisfied, complete, divinely fair.

In mercy, in goodness, how great is our King;
Our tribute, thanksgiving, with glad hearts we bring.
Thou art the Renewer, the Ancient of Days,
Who givest, for mourning, the garment of praise.

We thank Thee for work in the wide harvest field,
For gladness that ripens when sorrow is healed;
Made strong with Thy goodness that meets every need,
We gather the fruit of the Sower's good seed.

Dear Father and Saviour, we thank Thee for life,
And courage that rises undaunted by strife,
For confident giving and giving's reward,
For beauty and love in the life of our Lord.

In speechless prayer and reverence,
Dear Lord, I come to Thee;
My heart with love Thou fillest,
Yea, with humility.
My bread and wine Thou art,
With Thee I hold communion;
Thy presence healeth me.

To do Thy will is greater
Than sacrifice can be;
O give me needed courage
Sweet with sincerity.
From earthly thought released,
In speechless prayer and reverence,
Dear Lord, I come to Thee.

Luke 1:46
Maria Louise Baum

In Thee, my God and Saviour,
Forevermore the same,
My spirit hath rejoicing,
For holy is Thy name.
My soul doth magnify the Lord,
Sing all in glad accord!
Praise Him who lifts the lowly,
For faithful is His word.
I magnify and bless Thee,
For faithful is Thy word.

Thou who alone art mighty
Hast done to me great things.
Remembrance of Thy mercy
Sure help to Israel brings.
Thy power, O Lord, will I extol,
Who hast redeemed my soul;
I praise Thee, Lord, with gladness,
For Thou has made me whole.
I magnify and bless Thee,
For Thou hast made me whole.

In Thee, O Spirit true and tender,
I find my life as God's own child;
Within Thy light of glorious splendor
I lose the earth-clouds drear and wild.

Within Thy love is safe abiding
From every thought that giveth fear;
Within Thy truth a perfect chiding,
Should I forget that Thou art near.

In Thee I have no pain or sorrow,
No anxious thought, no load of care.
Thou art the same today, tomorrow;
Thy love and truth are everywhere.

Jesus' prayer for all his brethren:
Father, that they may be one,
Echoes down through all the ages,
Nor prayed he for these alone
But for all, that through all time
God's will be done.

One the Mind and Life of all things,
For we live in God alone;
One the Love whose ever-presence
Blesses all and injures none.
Safe within this Love we find all
being one.

Day by day the understanding
Of our oneness shall increase,
Till among all men and nations
Warfare shall forever cease,
So God's children all shall dwell
in joy and peace.

158
———
159

EDMUND H. SEARS
Adapted

It came upon the midnight clear,
That glorious song of old,
The angels, bending near the earth,
Their wondrous story told
Of peace on earth, good will to men,
From heaven's all-gracious King;
The world in solemn stillness lay
To hear the angels sing.

O ye beneath life's crushing load
Whose forms are bending low,
Who toil along the climbing way
With painful steps and slow;
Look now, for glad and golden hours
Come swiftly on the wing;
O rest beside the weary road,
And hear the angels sing.

For lo, the days are hastening on,
By prophets seen of old,
When with the ever-circling years
Shall come the time foretold;
When the new heaven and earth shall own
The Prince of Peace their King,
And all the world send back the song
Which now the angels sing.

It matters not what be thy lot,
So Love doth guide;
For storm or shine, pure peace is thine,
Whate'er betide.

And of these stones, or tyrants' thrones,
God able is
To raise up seed—in thought and deed—
To faithful His.

Aye, darkling sense, arise, go hence!
Our God is good.
False fears are foes—truth tatters those,
When understood.

Love looseth thee, and lifteth me,
Ayont hate's thrall:
There Life is light, and wisdom might,
And God is All.

The centuries break, the earth-bound wake,
God's glorified!
Who doth His will—His likeness still—
Is satisfied.

163

MARY A. LIVERMORE
Adapted

Jesus, what precept is like thine:
Forgive, as ye would be forgiven;
If heeded, O what power divine
Would then transform our earth to heaven.

So from our hearts must ever flow
A love that will all wrong outweigh;
Our lips must only blessings know,
And wrath and sin shall die away.

For it is Mind's most holy plan
To bring the wanderer back by love;
Then let us win our brother man,
And glorify our God above.

Isaac Watts
Adapted

164
165

Joy to the world, the Lord is come,
Let earth receive her King;
Let every heart prepare him room,
And heaven and nature sing.

No more let sin and sorrow grow,
Nor thorns infest the ground;
Where'er he comes, his blessings flow,
And hope and joy abound.

He rules the world with truth and grace,
And makes the nations prove
The glories of his righteousness
And wonders of his love.

166

167

HENRY FRANCIS LYTE
Adapted

Know, O child, thy full salvation;
Rise o'er sin and fear and care;
Joy to find, in every station,
Something still to do, or bear.

Think what spirit dwells within thee;
Think what Father's smiles are thine;
Think what Jesus did to win thee;
Child of heaven, can'st thou repine?

Haste thee on from grace to glory,
Armed with faith and winged with prayer;
Heaven's eternal day before thee,
God's own hand shall guide thee there.

So fulfill thy holy mission,
Swift shall pass thy pilgrim days,
Hope shall change to glad fruition,
Faith to sight and prayer to praise.

10TH CENTURY
RICHARD MANT, TR., *Adapted*

168

Let all the earth with songs rejoice;
Let heaven return the joyful voice;
All mindful of our God's great name,
Let every man His praise proclaim.

Ye servants who once bore the light
Of Gospel truth o'er darkest night,
Still may our work that light impart,
To glad the eyes and cheer the heart.

O God, by whom to them was given
The key that shuts and opens heaven,
Our chains unbind, our loss repair,
Reveal Thy power through answered prayer.

For at Thy will they preached the Word
Which cured disease, which health conferred:
And now, that healing power once more
Our peace and health to us restore.

Lead, kindly Light, amid the encircling gloom,
Lead Thou me on;
The night is dark, and I am far from home,
Lead Thou me on.
Keep Thou my feet; I do not ask to see
The distant scene; one step enough for me.

I was not ever thus, nor prayed that Thou
Shouldst lead me on;
I loved to choose and see my path; but now
Lead Thou me on.
I loved the garish day, and, spite of fears,
Pride ruled my will: remember not past years.

So long Thy power hath blest me, sure it still
Will lead me on
O'er moor and fen, o'er crag and torrent, till
The night is gone,
And with the morn those angel faces smile,
Which I have loved long since, and lost awhile.

JOHN GREENLEAF WHITTIER
Adapted

Let every creature hail the morn
On which the holy child was born
And know, through God's exceeding grace,
Release from things of time and place.
I listen, from no mortal tongue,
To hear the song the angels sung,
And wait within myself to know
The Christmas lilies bud and blow.

The outward symbols disappear
From him whose inward sight is clear,
And small must be the choice of days
To him who fills them all with praise.
Keep while ye need it, brothers mine,
With honest zeal your Christmas sign,
But judge not him who every morn
Feels in his heart the Lord Christ born.

Let us sing of Easter gladness
That rejoices every day,
Sing of hope and faith uplifted;
Love has rolled the stone away.
Lo, the promise and fulfillment,
Lo, the man whom God hath made,
Seen in glory of an Easter
Crowned with light that cannot fade.

When we touch Truth's healing garment
And behold Life's purity,
When we find in Love the refuge
That is man's security,
When we turn from earth to Spirit,
And from self have won release,
Then we see the risen Saviour;
Then we know his promised peace.

Living meekly as the Master,
Who of God was glorified,
Looking ever to the radiance
Of his wondrous Eastertide;
Freed of fear, of pain, and sorrow,
Giving God the honor due,
Every day will be an Easter
Filled with benedictions new.

Celia Thaxter
Adapted

Lift up thy light, O man, arise and shine,
Steadfast while loud the storms of life assail;
Immortal ray of that great Light divine,
'Gainst whose all-power no tempest shall prevail.

Hold high thy lamp above earth's restless tides,
Beacon of hope to those who watch afar.
Falsehood and fear shall pass, but Truth abides;
Thine be the splendor of her deathless star.

Should the world's sin and sorrow round thee rave,
Pierce thou the dark with Truth's undaunted ray,
Send out its light of joy to help and save,
That more and more shines to the perfect day.

173

CHRISTOPHER WORDSWORTH
Adapted

Love is kind and suffers long,
Love is meek and thinks no wrong,
Love than death itself more strong;
Therefore give us love.

Prophecy will fade away,
Melting in the light of day;
Love will ever with us stay;
Therefore give us love.

Faith will vanish into sight;
Hope shall be fulfilled in light;
Love will ever shine more bright;
Therefore give us love.

Faith and hope and love we see
Joining hand in hand agree;
But the greatest of the three,
And the best, is love.

Like as a mother, God comforteth His children;
Comfort is calm, that bids all tumult cease;
Comfort is hope and courage for endeavor,
Comfort is love, whose home abides in peace.

Love is true solace and giveth joy for sorrow,—
O, in that light, all earthly loss is gain;
Joy must endure, Love's giving is forever;
Life is of God, whose radiance cannot wane.

O holy presence, that stills all our demanding,
O love of God, that needs but to be known!
Heaven is at hand, when thy pure touch persuades us,
Comfort of God, that seeks and finds His own.

Lo, He sent His Word and healed them,
Still that Word of God is here.
Still its tender healing message
Speaks to every listening ear.
Truth divine, that overcometh
All the ills that seem to be,
In our hearts Thy Word abiding,
We may know Thee and be free

Love divine, that faileth never,
Still Thy presence and Thy power
Mighty are to save and heal us,
Guard and guide us every hour.
Life divine, Thy Word proclaimeth
All true being one with Thee.
Sinless, fearless, whole, rejoicing,
Now and through eternity.

Based on the Danish of
NIKOLAJ F. S. GRUNDTVIG

Long hast thou stood, O church of God,
Long mid the tempest's assailing,
Founded secure on timeless rock
Rises thy light, never failing;
Shining that all may understand
What has been wrought by God's command,
O'er night and chaos prevailing.

Let there be light, and light was there,
Clear as the Word that declared it;
Healing and peace to all it gave,
Who in humility shared it.
Ah, they were faithful, they who heard,
Steadfast their trust in God's great Word,
Steadfast the Love that prepared it.

Let there be light, the Word shines forth,
Lo, where the new morning whitens;
O church of God, with Book unsealed,
How its page beacons and brightens.
Living stones we, each in his place,
May we be worthy such a grace,
While Truth the wide earth enlightens.

177

THOMAS KELLY
Adapted

Look, ye saints, the day is breaking,
Joyful times are near at hand;
God, the mighty God, is speaking
By His Word in every land:
Day advances, day advances,
Darkness flees at His command.

God of Jacob, high and glorious,
Let Thy people see Thy power;
Let the gospel be victorious
Through the world forevermore:
Then shall every idol perish,
While Thy faithful saints adore.

Based on the Danish of
Nikolaj F. S. Grundtvig

Love is life's true crown and glory,
Love the splendor of the light,
Truly is God's counsel gentle,
Truly all His ways are bright;
Jesus knew the law of kindness,
Healing mind and heart of blindness;
And in heavenly wisdom taught
Holy works of love he wrought.

Love, the Golden Rule of living,
Showeth forth the perfect Mind;
Love, our debt to God who gives it,
All compassion is, and kind;
Charity the law fulfilleth,
Mid the nations rancor stilleth;
Loving hearts in friendship blend,
One in Him, our heavenly Friend.

Love one another,—word of revelation;
Love frees from error's thrall,—Love is liberation.
Love's way the Master trod;
He that loves shall walk with God.
Love is the royal way.

Love knows no evil, neither shade of sadness;
Love casts out every fear, lifts the heart to gladness.
Love heals our every ill,
All the law does love fulfill.
Love is our answered prayer.

Love now is dawning over every nation;
Showing true brotherhood, publishing salvation,
Love bids all discord cease.
Conquering hate, enthroning peace,
Love, Love alone is power.

Based on the Danish of
Jens N. L. Schjørring

Love the Lord thy God:
Love is staff and rod
For heart and soul and mind.
In this command forever strong,
To silence thoughts of wrong
All laws fulfillment find.

Here we rest content:
Good from God is sent
Where seeds of Love are sown.
Who as himself his neighbor loves,
By constant purpose proves
His neighbor's good his own.

They whose every thought
Still from Love is sought,
In Soul, not flesh, abide.
Love's presence gives a joy untold:
Now may we all behold
The Spirit and the bride.

Loving Father, we Thy children
Look to Thee in fear’s dark night
While the angels of Thy presence
Guide us upward to the light.

Then we feel the power that lifts us
To Thy holy secret place,
Where our gloom is lost in glory
As we see Thee face to face.

We would learn, O gracious Father,
To reflect Thy healing love.
May we all awake to praise Thee
For Thy good gifts from above.

Make us strong to bear the message
To Thy children far and near:
Fear shall have no more dominion.
God is All, and heaven is here.

Make channels for the streams of Love,
Where they may broadly run;
And Love has overflowing streams,
To fill them every one.

But if at any time we cease
Such channels to provide,
The very founts of love for us
Will then seem parched and dried.

For we must share, if we would keep
That blessing from above;
They cease to have who cease to give:
Such is the law of Love.

183

184

HORATIUS BONAR
Adapted

Make haste, O man, to do
Whatever must be done;
Thou hast no time to lose in sloth,
When all to Truth must come.

The useful and the great,
The thing that never dies,
The silent toil that is not lost,—
Set these before thine eyes.

Up, face the task and work;
Fling ease and self away;
This is no time for thee to sleep;
Up, watch, and work, and pray.

Master and Lord, 'tis good to be here,
Guided by thee to joy-crowned height
Where we man's perfect sonship see
Safe and secure in radiant light.

Light of the world, 'tis good to hold fast
To the clear vision thou hast shown;
So shall this vision gently mold
Our lives more closely to thine own.

Thou art the Way, we know that the truth
Shown on the mountain here above,
Still in thy light's triumphant glow
Through all earth's valleys we can prove.

186
187

William Gaskell
Adapted

Mighty God, the First, the Last,
What are ages in Thy sight
But as yesterday when past,
Or a watch within the night?

All that being e'er shall know,
On, still on, through farthest years,
All eternity can show,
Bright before Thee now appears.

Whatsoe'er our lot may be,
Calmly in this thought we rest:
When we see as Thou dost see,
We shall love Thee and be blest.

No eye hath seen, nor tongue declared,
Nor hath it entered heart of man,
To know what God hath here prepared
For them that love and trust His plan.

But He whose Spirit searcheth deep
Hath sent His Word to all mankind,
The Word that bids them find and keep
The priceless treasures of His Mind.

O come and find, the Spirit saith,
The Truth that maketh all men free.
The world is sad with dreams of death.
Lo, I am Life, come unto Me.

Psalm 121

From Swedish Version

Mine eyes look toward the mountains,
Help cometh from on high;
From God who never slumbers,
Whose care is ever nigh.
My foot shall not be moved,
My keeper is the Lord,
He never shall forsake me;
I trust me to His Word.

God keepeth me from falling,
Fulfilleth all my need;
His love doth e'er uphold me
In faithful word and deed.
He keepeth me from evil,
My onward way doth trace,
My going and my coming
He crowneth with His grace.

Frederic Mann
By permission of A. W. Ridley & Co., Adapted

190
191

My God, my Father, make me strong,
When tasks of life seem hard and long,
To greet them with this triumph song,
Thy will be done.

With confident and humble mind,
My joy in service I would find,
My prayer through every task assigned,
Thy will be done.

Things deemed impossible I dare,
Thine is the call and Thine the care,
Thy wisdom shall the way prepare;
Thy will be done.

Heaven's music chimes the glad days in,
Hope soars beyond death, pain and sin,
Faith sings in triumph, Love doth win;
Thy will is done.

Nearer, my God, to Thee,
Nearer to Thee:
E'en though it be a cross
That raiseth me;
Still all my song shall be,

REFRAIN
Nearer, my God, to Thee,
Nearer, my God, to Thee,
Nearer to Thee.

Though like the wanderer,
The sun gone down,
Darkness be over me,
My rest a stone;
Yet in my dreams I'd be

REFRAIN

— continued on next page —

There let the way appear,
Steps unto heaven;
All that Thou sendest me
In mercy given;
Angels to beckon me

REFRAIN

Then, with my waking thoughts
Bright with Thy praise,
Out of my stony griefs
Bethel I'll raise;
So by my woes to be

REFRAIN

Or if on joyful wing
Cleaving the sky,
Sun, moon, and stars forgot,
Upward I fly,
Still all my song shall be,

REFRAIN

No mortal sense can still or stay
The flight of silent prayer,
Unceasing, voiceless, heart desire
That seeks God everywhere.

The heart's own longing lifts it high
Where words can never reach,
Though human lips may never form
That glory into speech.

The voices that are worldly wise,
With mortal modes in tune,
Are mute in that transcendent hour
When God and man commune.

Not what I am, O Lord, but what Thou art;
That, that alone can be my soul's true rest;
Thy love, not mine, bids fear and doubt depart,
And stills the tumult of my troubled breast.

Girt with the love of God, on every side,
I breathe that love as heaven's own healing air;
I work and pray, and follow still my guide,
And fear no foe, escaping every snare.

'Tis what I know of Thee, my Lord and God,
That fills my soul with peace, my lips with song;
Thou art my health, my joy, my staff, my rod;
I lean on Thee, in weakness I am strong.

Now is the time approaching,
By prophets long foretold,
When all shall dwell together,
One Shepherd and one fold.
Now Jew and Gentile, meeting
From many a distant shore,
Around one altar kneeling,
One common Lord adore.

Let all that now divides us
Remove and pass away,
Like shadows of the morning
Before the blaze of day.
Let all that now unites us
More sweet and lasting prove,
A closer bond of union,
In a blest land of love.

Now sweeping down the years untold,
The day of Truth is breaking;
And sweet and fair the leaves unfold,
Of Love's immortal waking.

For flower and fruitage now are seen,
Where blight and mildew rested:
The Christ today to us has been
By word and deed attested.

His living presence we have felt,
The Word made flesh among us:
And hearts of stone before him melt,
His peace is brooding o'er us.

199

Martin Rinkart
Catherine Winkworth, Tr., *Adapted*

Now thank we all our God
With grateful hearts and voices
Who wondrous things hath done,
In whom the world rejoices;
Who from the days of yore
Hath blessed us on our way
With countless gifts of love
And still is ours today.

We know our gracious God
Through all our life is near us,
To fill our thoughts with light,
To strengthen us and cheer us;
From His eternal care
We never shall remove,
Encompassed by His grace,
Enfolded in His love.

O daughter of Zion, awake from thy sadness;
Awake, for thy foes shall oppress thee no more;
And bright o'er thy hills dawns the daystar of gladness;
Arise, for the night of thy sorrow is o'er.

O many thy foes, but the arm that subdued them
And scattered their legions was mightier far;
They fled like the chaff from the scourge that pursued them,
For vain were their steeds and their chariots of war.

O daughter of Zion, the power that hath saved thee,
Extolled with the harp and the timbrel should be;
Then shout, for the foe is destroyed that enslaved thee;
Th' oppressor is vanquished, and Zion is free.

O do not bar your mind
Against the light of good;
But open wide, let in the Word,
And Truth will be your food.

Truth will from error free
Your long enslaved mind,
And bring the light of liberty
Where it shall be enshrined.

Hid treasures it reveals
To all who know its power;
And all who will may light receive
In this most gracious hour.

Then open wide your heart
To Truth and Light and Love;
You then shall know your life is hid
With Christ in God above.

O dreamer, leave thy dreams for joyful waking,
O captive, rise and sing, for thou art free;
The Christ is here, all dreams of error breaking,
Unloosing bonds of all captivity.

He comes to bless thee on his wings of healing;
To banish pain, and wipe all tears away;
He comes anew, to humble hearts revealing
The mounting footsteps of the upward way.

He comes to give thee joy for desolation,
Beauty for ashes of the vanished years;
For every tear to bring full compensation,
To give thee confidence for all thy fears.

He comes to call the dumb to joyful singing;
The deaf to hear; the blinded eyes to see;
The glorious tidings of salvation bringing.
O captive, rise, thy Saviour comes to thee.

O Father, may we bear each hour
The flag of hope and peace unfurled,
And mirror forth Love's sacred power
To feed and bless a hungry world.
We shall not falter by the way
If we but place our trust in Thee,
Obeying gladly day by day
The living Truth that makes men free.

Help us to know that all is well
E'en though we wander through earth's shade,
To know that all Thy children dwell
Within Love's stronghold unafraid.
Teach us to follow fearlessly
The way our gentle Master trod,
'Twill lead us safely home to Thee,
O loving Father-Mother, God.

Based on the Swedish of
LINA SANDELL BERG

O Father, Thy kingdom is come upon earth,
Thou rulest in all Thy creation;
Thou sendest Thy witnesses, telling Thy worth,
To call and entreat every nation,
With news of Thy mighty salvation.

They lift up a light amid shadows of fear,
And Love is Thy banner above them;
No trouble shall touch them, no foes that appear
Shall e'er from their loyalty move them;
'Tis Thou dost uphold and approve them.

They go in Thy strength, and they speak in Thy name,
With power of Thy promise forth faring,
And during the battle the victory claim,—
Their trust in Thy truth is their daring,
Salvation to all men declaring.

O for a faith that will not shrink,
Though pressed by every foe;
That will not tremble on the brink
Of any earthly woe;

A faith that shines more bright and clear
When tempests rage without;
That when in danger knows no fear,
In darkness feels no doubt;

O, give us such a faith as this,
And then, whate'er may come,
We taste e'en here the hallowed bliss
Of our eternal home.

O God, our Father-Mother, Love,
Purge Thou our hearts from sin,
That in Thy radiancy divine
We may with eyes undimmed define
Thy will, reality.

O God, our Father-Mother, Truth,
Send forth Thy light sublime,
That in its pure and cleansing rays
We may, with thought attuned to praise,
Behold reality.

O God, our Father-Mother, Life,
Reveal in us Thy might,
That henceforth we may live to Thee,
In all our ways reflecting Thee,
And know reality.

207
—*to*—
212

Mother's Evening Prayer

Mary Baker Eddy

O gentle presence, peace and joy and power;
O Life divine, that owns each waiting hour,
Thou Love that guards the nestling's faltering flight!
Keep Thou my child on upward wing tonight.

Love is our refuge; only with mine eye
Can I behold the snare, the pit, the fall:
His habitation high is here, and nigh,
His arm encircles me, and mine, and all.

O make me glad for every scalding tear,
For hope deferred, ingratitude, disdain!
Wait, and love more for every hate, and fear
No ill,—since God is good, and loss is gain.

Beneath the shadow of His mighty wing;
In that sweet secret of the narrow way,
Seeking and finding, with the angels sing:
"Lo, I am with you alway,"—watch and pray.

No snare, no fowler, pestilence or pain;
No night drops down upon the troubled breast,
When heaven's aftersmile earth's tear-drops gain,
And mother finds her home and heav'nly rest.

O God, our help in ages past,
Our hope for time to come,
Our shelter from the stormy blast,
And our eternal home.

Before the hills in order stood,
Or earth received her frame,
From everlasting Thou art God,
To endless years the same.

A thousand ages in Thy sight
Are like an evening gone,
Short as the watch that ends the night
Before the rising sun.

O God, our help in ages past,
Our hope for time to come,
Thou art our guard while ages last,
And our eternal home.

NATHANIEL L. FROTHINGHAM
Adapted

O God, whose presence glows in all,
Within, around us, and above,
Thy Word we bless, Thy name we call,
Whose Word is Truth, whose name is Love.

May Love its holy influence pour
To keep us meek, and make us free;
And bind its tender blessing more
Round each with all, and all with Thee.

O send its angel to our side,
Its holy calm upon the breast;
For we would know no other guide,
And we can need no other rest.

O happy is the man who hears
Instruction's warning voice;
And who celestial wisdom makes
His early, only choice.

For she has treasures greater far
Than east or west unfold;
And her rewards more precious are
Than all their stores of gold.

According as her labors rise,
So her rewards increase;
Her ways are ways of pleasantness,
And all her paths are peace.

From the German of
GEORG NEUMARK

O he who trusts in God's protection
And hopes in Him when fears alarm,
Is sheltered by His loving-kindness,
Delivered by His mighty arm;
If ye God's law can understand,
Ye have not builded on the sand.

O wait on Him with veneration,
Be silent in humility;
He leads you after His own counsel,
His will is done and still shall be;
All good for you His wisdom planned;
O trust in God and understand.

O, he whom Jesus loved has truly spoken,
That holier worship, which God deigns to bless,
Restores the lost, and heals the spirit broken,
And feeds the widow and the fatherless.

Then, brother man, fold to thy heart thy brother,
For where love dwells, the peace of God is there:
To worship rightly is to love each other;
Each smile a hymn, each kindly deed a prayer.

Follow with reverent steps the great example
Of him whose holy work was doing good;
So shall the wide earth seem our Father's temple,
Each loving life a psalm of gratitude.

O Life that maketh all things new,
The blooming earth, the thoughts of men;
Our pilgrim feet, wet with Thy dew,
In gladness hither turn again.

From hand to hand the greeting flows,
From eye to eye the signals run,
From heart to heart the bright hope glows,
The seekers of the Light are one:

One in the freedom of the truth,
One in the joy of paths untrod,
One in the heart's perennial youth,
One in the larger thought of God;—

The freer step, the fuller breath,
The wide horizon's grander view;
The sense of Life that knows no death,—
The Life that maketh all things new.

O Jesus, our dear Master,
Thy works, now understood,
Reveal their full effulgence
Through love and brotherhood.
Today Christ's precious Science
Thy healing power makes plain:
With joy may all obey thee
And cast out sin and pain.

The Christ, eternal manhood,
As God's own Son beloved,
A tender ever-presence
Within each heart is proved.
O God, our Father-Mother,
Thy name we see expressed
By man, who in Thy Science
Is perfect, holy, blessed.

O Science, God-sent message
To tired humanity,
Thou art Love's revelation
Of Truth that makes us free.
Thy kingdom, God, within us
Shows forth Love's sweet control.
God's idea, man, rejoices;
He knows the reign of Soul.

O little town of Bethlehem,
How still we see thee lie;
Above thy deep and dreamless sleep
The silent stars go by;
Yet in thy dark streets shineth
The everlasting Light;
The hopes and fears of all the years
Are met in thee tonight.

O morning stars, together
Proclaim the holy birth,
And praises sing to God the King,
And peace to men on earth;
Where charity stands watching
And faith holds wide the door,
The dark night wakes, the glory breaks,
And Christmas comes once more.

How silently, how silently,
The wondrous gift is given;
So God imparts to human hearts
The blessings of His heaven.
No ear may hear his coming,
But in this world of sin,
Where meekness will receive him, still
The dear Christ enters in.

John Ryland
Adapted

O Lord, I would delight in Thee,
And on Thy care depend;
To Thee in every trouble flee,
My best, my ever Friend.
When all material streams are dried,
Thy fullness is the same;
May I with this be satisfied,
And glory in Thy name.

All good, where'er it may be found,
Its source doth find in Thee;
I must have all things and abound,
While God is God to me.
O that I had a stronger faith,
To look within the veil,
To credit what my Saviour saith,
Whose word can never fail.

He that has made my heaven secure,
Will here all good provide;
While Christ is rich, can I be poor?
What can I want beside?
O God, I cast my care on Thee;
I triumph and adore;
Henceforth my great concern shall be
To love and praise Thee more.

O Lord of life, to Thee we lift
Our hearts in praise for those,
Thy prophets, who have shown Thy gift
Of grace that ever grows,
Of truth that spreads from shore to shore,
Of wisdom's widening ray,
Of light that shineth more and more
Unto Thy perfect day.

Shine forth, O Light, that we may see,
With hearts all unafraid,
The meaning and the majesty
Of things that Thou hast made:
Shine forth, and let the darkling past
Beneath Thy beam grow bright;
Shine forth, and touch the future vast
With Thine untroubled light.

Light up Thy word; the fettered page
From darkened bondage free:
Light up our way; lead forth this age
In love's large liberty.
O Light of light, within us dwell,
Through us Thy radiance pour,
That word and deed Thy truths may tell,
And praise Thee evermore.

William Cowper
Adapted

227

O Lord, where'er Thy people meet,
There they behold Thy mercy seat;
Where'er they seek Thee, Thou art found,
And every place is hallowed ground.

For Thou, within no walls confined,
Dwellest with them of humble mind;
Such ever bring Thee where they come;
And where Thou art they find their home.

Here we may prove the power of prayer
To strengthen faith and sweeten care;
To teach our faint desires to rise,
And bring all heaven before our eyes.

O Love divine, that dwells serene,
Whose light of life has no eclipse,
We feel Thy comfort, though unseen,
And lay our hand upon our lips.

No words our hidden joy can tell,
A welling fount, it fills the heart;
Not in the flesh, in Thee we dwell,
In Thee our life, for Life Thou art.

With love we meet the low despite
Of such as hate our Master's way.
With patience he maintained the right;
So may we triumph day by day.

O Love divine, whose constant beam
Shines on the eyes that will not see,
And waits to bless us while we dream,
Nor leav'st us though we turn from Thee.
Nor bounds, nor clime, nor creed Thou know'st,
Wide as our need Thy favors fall;
The white wings of the Holy Ghost
Stoop unseen o'er the heads of all.

O Truth which sage and prophet saw,
Long sought without, but found within,
The rule of Love beyond all law,
The Life o'ercoming death and sin,
O shine on us with light which glowed
Upon the waiting shepherds' way,
Who saw the darkness overflowed
With tides of everlasting day.

O Love, O Life, our faith and sight
Thy presence maketh one;
As, through transfigured clouds of white,
We trace the noonday sun.

We faintly hear, we dimly see,
In differing phrase we pray;
But, dim or clear, we own in Thee
The Light, the Truth, the Way.

To do Thy will is more than praise,
As words are less than deeds;
And simple trust can find Thy ways
We miss with chart of creeds.

Our friend, our brother, and our Lord,
What may thy service be?
Nor name, nor form, nor ritual word,
But simply following thee.

O Love, our Mother, ever near,
To Thee we turn from doubt and fear!
In perfect peace our thoughts abide;
Our hearts now in this truth confide:
Man is the child of God.

O Light, in Thy light we can see
That man is ever one with Thee.
In love our lives Thou dost enfold,
And now our waiting hopes behold
That man is God's own child.

O joy that ever will remain,
Midst seeming sorrow, hate, and pain,
Our hearts to fill with this glad song
That soars above the mists of wrong:
Man is the loved of Love.

O Love whose perfect path is known
To all who walk the ways of God,
Whose mysteries are so clearly shown
To pilgrims with the gospel shod;

Thy radiance is so pure, so free,
So beautiful and swift to bless,
That by reflection constantly
We manifest Thy tenderness:

And every sacred shrine shall burn
With flames of Truth divinely bright,
And every weary child shall turn
In gratitude toward Thee, the Light.

234
———
235

O Master, let me walk with thee
In lowly paths of service free;
Tell me thy secret; help me bear
The strain of toil, the fret of care.

Help me the slow of heart to move
By some clear winning word of love;
Teach me the wayward feet to stay,
And guide them in the homeward way.

Teach me thy patience; still with thee
In closer, dearer company,
In work that keeps faith sweet and strong,
In trust that triumphs over wrong.

In hope that sends a shining ray
Far down the future's broadening way;
In peace that God alone can give,
With thee, O Master, let me live.

O peace of the world, O hope in each breast,
O Bethlehem star that ages have blest,
A day of fresh promise breaks over the land,
Gaunt warfare is doomed, and God's kingdom at hand!

From cannon and sword shape tillers of soil,
No more let dire hate man's spirit despoil,
Let Truth be proclaimed, let God's love be retold,
That men of good will may their brethren uphold.

As stars in their courses never contend,
As blossoms their hues in harmony blend,
As bird voices mingle in joyful refrain,
So God's loving children in concord remain.

Our God is one Mind, the Mind we adore;
Ineffable joy His love doth outpour;
Let nations be one in a union of love,
God's bountiful peace, all earth's treasures above.

O may we be still and seek Him,
Seek with consecration whole,
Listening thus to hear the message,
Far from sense and hid in Soul.

He hath promised we shall find Him,
Love divine its promise keeps;
God is watching with the watchful,
God is Life that never sleeps.

If we pray to Him in secret,
Lift to Him the heart's desire,
We shall find our earthly longings
All made pure by Love's pure fire.

Then upon the precious metal
God's own image will appear,
Faithfully to Him reflected,
One with Him forever near.

O, sometimes gleams upon our sight,
Through present wrong, th' eternal right;
And step by step, since time began,
We see the steady gain of man.

For all of good the past hath had
Remains to make our own time glad,
Our common, daily life divine,
And every land a Palestine.

Through the harsh noises of our day,
A low sweet prelude finds its way;
Through clouds of doubt and creeds of fear
A light is breaking, calm and clear.

Henceforth my heart shall sigh no more
For olden time and holier shore:
God's love and blessing, then and there,
Are now and here and everywhere.

BENJAMIN BEDDOME
Adapted

240
241

O Spirit, source of light,
Thy grace is unconfined;
Dispel the gloomy shades of night,
Reveal the light of Mind.

Now to our eyes display
The truth Thy words reveal;
Cause us to run the heavenly way,
Delighting in Thy will.

Thy teachings make us know
The mysteries of Thy love;
The vanity of things below,
The joy of things above.

O, still in accents sweet and strong
Sounds forth the ancient word:
More reapers for white harvest fields,
More laborers for the Lord.

We hear the call; no more in dreams
And selfish ease we lie,
But girded for our Father's work,
Go forth beneath His sky.

O Thou whose call our hearts hath stirred,
To do Thy will we come,
Thrust in our sickles at Thy word,
And bear our harvest home.

O sweet and tender as the dawn,
With mighty power to heal and bless,
Is God's dear gift to all His own:
The happy grace of gentleness.

How quickly burdens fall away,
How hearts grow light, rejoice, are glad,
When Love with touch of gentleness
Uplifts the sinning and the sad.

This gentle grace of Love divine
Is sweet as breath of opening flower.
Self-love and harshness disappear
Beneath its tender, healing power.

O tender, loving Shepherd,
We long to follow thee,
To follow where thou leadest,
Though rough the path may be;
Though dark and heavy shadows
Enshroud the way with gloom,
We know that Love will guide us,
And safely lead us home.

We know, beloved Shepherd,
The path that thou hast trod
Leads ever out of darkness,
And on and up to God.
If from that path we wander,
And far astray we roam,
O, call us, faithful Shepherd,
And bring us safely home.

Throughout the way, dear Shepherd,
Thy strong hand doth uphold;
The weary ones, at nightfall,
Thou gently dost enfold.
And when to Truth's green pastures
With joy at length we come,
There shall we find, O Shepherd,
Our blest, eternal home.

O Thou who spreadest the heaven like a tent,
He who depends on Thee, ne'er is forspent,
Still for his might on Thee he ever counteth,
On wings of eagles he, unwearied, mounteth.

REFRAIN

Have ye not heard, have ye not known
The everlasting God
Creator is of heaven and earth,
And He alone is Lord.

So shall the glory of God be revealed,
All flesh shall see it and all shall be healed;
In word and deed declare Him and adore Him.
God's will is done, and all is plain before Him.

REFRAIN

O walk with God along the road,
Your strength He will renew;
Wait on the everlasting God,
And He will walk with you.

Ye shall not to your daily task
Without your God repair,
But on your work His blessing ask
And prove His glory there.

Ye shall not faint, ye shall not fail;
In Spirit ye are strong;
Each task divine ye still shall hail,
And blend it with a song.

O, when we see God's mercy
Widespread in every place
And know how flows the fountain
Of His unbounded grace,
Can we withhold a tribute,
Forbear a psalm to raise,
Or leave unsung one blessing,
In this our hymn of praise?

Our gratitude is riches,
Complaint is poverty,
Our trials bloom in blessings,
They test our constancy.
O, life from joy is minted,
An everlasting gold,
True gladness is the treasure
That grateful hearts will hold.

251
252

WILLIAM W. HOW
Adapted

O Word of God, most holy,
O wisdom from on high,
O Truth, unchanged, unchanging,
O light of earth's dark sky,
We bless Thee for the radiance
That from the hallowed page,
A lantern to our footsteps,
Shines on from age to age.

O Word of God the Father,
Thou art the gift divine,
And still thy light is lifted,
O'er all the lands to shine.
It is the chart and compass
To guide us to our Lord;
It is the heaven-drawn picture
Of Christ, the living Word.

O'er waiting harpstrings of the mind
There sweeps a strain,
Low, sad, and sweet, whose measures bind
The power of pain,

And wake a white-winged angel throng
Of thoughts, illumed
By faith, and breathed in raptured song,
With love perfumed.

Then His unveiled, sweet mercies show
Life's burdens light.
I kiss the cross, and wake to know
A world more bright.

And o'er earth's troubled, angry sea
I see Christ walk,
And come to me, and tenderly,
Divinely talk.

Thus Truth engrounds me on the rock,
Upon Life's shore,
'Gainst which the winds and waves can shock,
Oh, nevermore!

— *continued on next page* —

From tired joy and grief afar,
And nearer Thee,—
Father, where Thine own children are,
I love to be.

My prayer, some daily good to do
To Thine, for Thee;
An offering pure of Love, whereto
God leadeth me.

Oft to every man and nation
Comes the moment to decide,
In the strife of Truth with falsehood,
For the good or evil side.
A great cause, God's new Messiah,
Shows to each the bloom or blight,
So can choice be made by all men
Twixt the darkness and the light.

New occasions teach new duties,
Time makes ancient creeds uncouth;
They must upward still and onward
Who would keep abreast of Truth,
And serenely down the future
See the thought of men incline
To the side of perfect justice
And to God's supreme design.

Though the cause of evil prosper,
Yet 'tis Truth alone is strong;
Though her portion be the scaffold,
And upon the throne be wrong,
Yet that scaffold sways the future,
And behind the dim unknown
Standeth God within the shadow
Keeping watch above His own.

One cup of healing oil and wine,
One offering laid on mercy's shrine,
Is thrice more grateful, Lord, to Thee,
Than lifted eye or bended knee.

In true and inward faith we trace
The source of every outward grace;
Within the pious heart it plays,
A living fount of joy and praise.

Kind deeds of peace and love betray
Where'er the stream has found its way;
But where these spring not rich and fair,
The stream has never wandered there.

FREDERICK L. HOSMER
Adapted

260

One thought I have, my ample creed,
So deep it is and broad,
And equal to my every need,—
It is the thought of God.

Each morn unfolds His blessings new,
I take in trust my road;
And rising freshly to my view,
Shines forth the thought of God.

To this their secret strength they owed,
The martyr's path who trod;
The fountains of their patience flowed
From out their thought of God.

Be still the light upon my way,
My pilgrim staff and rod,
My rest by night, my strength by day,
O blessed thought of God.

One holy church of God appears
Through every age and race,
Unwasted by the lapse of years,
Unchanged by changing place.

From oldest time, on farthest shores,
Beneath the pine or palm,
One unseen presence she adores,
With silence or with psalm.

Her priests are all God's faithful sons,
To serve the world raised up;
The pure in heart her baptized ones;
Love, her communion cup.

From the Swedish of
J. O. Wallin

Only God can bring us gladness,
Only God can give us peace;
Joys are vain that end in sadness,
Joy divine shall never cease.
Mid the shade of want and sorrow
Undisturbed, our hearts rejoice;
Patient, wait the brighter morrow;
Faithful, heed the Father's voice.

As the stars in order going,
All harmonious, He doth move;
Heavenly calm and comfort showing,
Comes the healing word of Love.
Who the word of wisdom heareth
Feels the Father Love within,
Where as dawn the shadow cleareth,
Love outshines the night of sin.

So we find the true atonement,
Know in God the perfect Friend;
For in Love is our at-one-ment,
Where all hearts in Him may blend.
Here from prisoning pain and sorrow
Have we all a sure release,
Only God can bring us gladness,
Only God can give us peace.

Onward, Christian soldiers,
Marching as to war,
With the cross of Jesus
Going on before.
Christ, the royal Master,
Leads against the foe;
Forward into battle,
See his banners go.

REFRAIN

Onward, Christian soldiers,
Marching as to war,
With the cross of Jesus
Going on before.

Like a mighty army,
Moves the Church of God;
Brothers, we are treading
Where the saints have trod;
We are not divided,
All one body we,
One in hope and doctrine,
One in charity.

REFRAIN

— *continued on next page* —

Crowns and thrones may perish,
Kingdoms rise and wane,
But the Church of Jesus
Constant will remain;
Gates of hell can never
'Gainst that Church prevail;
We have Christ's own promise,
And that cannot fail.

REFRAIN

Onward, then, ye people,
Join our happy throng;
Blend with ours your voices
In the triumph song;
Glory, laud and honor
Unto Christ the King;
This through countless ages
Men and angels sing.

REFRAIN

265

Samuel Johnson
Adapted

Onward, Christian, though the region
Where thou art seem drear and lone;
God hath set a guardian legion
Very near thee, press thou on.

By the Christ road, and none other,
Is the mount of vision won;
Tread it with rejoicing, brother:
Jesus trod it, press thou on.

By thy trustful, calm endeavor,
Guiding, cheering, like the sun,
Earth-bound hearts thou shalt deliver;
O, for their sake, press thou on.

Attributed to Thomas Cotterill
Adapted

Our God is Love, and all His sons
His image bear, we know;
The heart with love to God inspired,
With love to man will glow.

Teach us to love each other, Lord,
As we are loved by Thee;
None who are truly born of God
Can live in enmity.

Heirs of the same immortal bliss,
Our hopes and aims the same,
In bonds of love our hearts unite,
To praise His holy name.

So may we all with one accord
Learn how true Christians love;
And glorify our Father's grace,
And seek that grace to prove.

Emily F. Seal

Our God is All-in-all,
His children cannot fear;
See baseless evil fall,
And know that God is here.

Our God is All; in space
No subtle error creeps;
We see Truth's glowing face,
And Love that never sleeps.

We see creative Mind,
The Principle, the Life;
And Soul and substance find,
But never discord, strife.

O, Perfect and Divine,
We hear Thy loving call,
And seek no earthly shrine
But crown Thee Lord of all.

269
270

Our God is Love, unchanging Love,
And can we ask for more?
Our prayer for Love's increase is vain;
'Twas infinite before.
Ask not the Lord with breath of praise
For more than we accept;
The open fount is free to all,
God's promises are kept.

Our God is Mind, the perfect Mind,
Intelligence divine;
Shall mortal man ask Him to change
His infinite design?
The heart that yearns for righteousness,
With longing unalloyed,
In such desire sends up a prayer
That ne'er returneth void.

O loving Father, well we know
That words alone are vain,
That those who seek Thy will to do,
The true communion gain.
Then may our deeds our pure desire
For growth in grace express,
That we may know how Love divine
Forever waits to bless.

271/272

Isaac Watts
Adapted

Our God shall reign where'er the sun
Does his successive journeys run;
His kingdom stretch from shore to shore,
Till moons shall wax and wane no more.

All people shall with joyful tongue
Dwell on His love with sweetest song,
And infant voices shall proclaim
Their early blessings on His name.

For blessings flow where'er He reigns;
The prisoner leaps to loose his chains,
The weary find eternal rest,
And all the sons of want are blest.

Let every creature rise, and bring
Peculiar honors to our King;
Let angel songs be heard again
And earth repeat the long Amen.

Partners of a glorious hope,
Lift your hearts and voices up;
Nobly let us bear the strife,
Keep the holiness of life.

Still forget the things behind,
Follow God, the only Mind,
To the mark unwearied press,
Seize the crown of righteousness.

In our lives our faith be known,
Faith by holy actions shown;
Faith that mountains can remove,
Faith that always works by love.

Praise now creative Mind,
Maker of earth and heaven;
Glory and power to Him belong,
Joy of the sun and skies,
Strength where the hills arise,
So let us praise with joy and song.

Ages have seen His might,
Father we call His name;
Nights of our mourning and sorrow end,
Light blesses opened eyes,
Joys like the dawns arise
As we see Him our God and Friend.

Saviour from death is He;
Life is our heritage;
Mercy and goodness forever guide;
Ours is the risen Christ,
Daily we keep our tryst,
And evermore in Love confide.

Peace be to this congregation;
Peace to every heart therein;
Peace, the earnest of salvation;
Peace, the fruit of conquered sin;
Peace, that speaks the heavenly Giver;
Peace, to worldly minds unknown;
Peace, that floweth as a river
From th' eternal source alone.

O Thou God of peace, be near us,
Fix within our hearts Thy home;
With Thy bright appearing cheer us,
In Thy blessed freedom come.
Come with all Thy revelations,
Truth which we so long have sought;
Come with Thy deep consolations,
Peace of God which passeth thought.

278
279

P. M.
Adapted

Pilgrim on earth, home and heaven are within thee,
Heir of the ages and child of the day.
Cared for, watched over, beloved and protected,
Walk thou with courage each step of the way.

Truthful and steadfast though trials betide thee,
Ever one thing do thou ask of thy Lord,
Grace to go forward, wherever He guide thee,
Gladly obeying the call of His word.

Healed is thy hardness, His love hath dissolved it,
Full is the promise, the blessing how kind;
So shall His tenderness teach thee compassion,
So all the merciful, mercy shall find.

Praise, my soul, the King of heaven;
To His feet thy tribute bring.
Ransomed, healed, restored, forgiven,
Who like us His praise should sing?
Praise Him, praise Him, praise Him,
praise Him,
Praise the everlasting King.

Fatherlike, He tends and spares us,
Well our daily needs He knows;
In His hand He gently bears us,
Rescues us from all our foes.
Praise Him, praise Him, praise Him,
praise Him,
Widely as His mercy flows.

Praise Him for His grace and favor
To our fathers in distress;
Praise Him still the same forever,
Slow to chide, and swift to bless.
Praise Him, praise Him, praise Him,
praise Him,
Glorious in His faithfulness.

281

Harriet Auber
Adapted

Praise our great and gracious Lord,
Call upon His holy name;
Strains of joy tune every chord,
All His mighty acts proclaim.
How He leads His chosen
Unto Canaan's promised land,
How the Word we have heard
Firm and changeless still shall stand.

He has given the cloud by day,
Given the moving fire by night;
Guides His Israel on their way
From the darkness into light.
He it is who grants us
Sure retreat and refuge nigh.
Light of dawn leads us on,
'Tis the dayspring from on high.

Praise the Lord, ye heavens, adore Him;
Praise Him, angels, in the height;
Sun and moon, rejoice before Him,
Praise Him, all ye stars of light;
Praise the Lord, for He hath spoken,
Worlds His mighty voice obeyed;
Laws that never shall be broken
For their guidance hath He made.

Praise the Lord, for He is glorious;
Never shall His promise fail;
God hath made His saints victorious,
Sin and death shall not prevail.
Praise the God of our salvation;
Hosts on high, His power proclaim;
Heaven and earth, and all creation,
Laud and magnify His name.

283

From the German of
Joachim Neander

Praise we the Lord, for His mercy endureth forever.
Let us extol Him with joyous and loving endeavor;
Come let us sing,
Praising our God and our King,
Should we be silent? Ah, never.

Praise we the Lord, who our footsteps still
holdeth from sliding;
Daily He campeth about us, protecting and
guiding;
E'en while we sleep
Watch doth He tenderly keep;
Ever new mercies providing.

Praise we the Lord with a joyous and glad
adoration;
Lo, unto them that believe there is no
condemnation;
Now will we raise
Songs of thanksgiving and praise,
Christ is become our salvation.

Prayer is the heart's sincere desire,
Uttered or unexpressed;
The motion of a hidden fire
That trembles in the breast.

Prayer is the simplest form of speech
That infant lips can try;
And prayer's sublimest strain doth reach
The Majesty on high.

Prayer is the Christian's vital breath,
The Christian's native air:
His watchword, overcoming death:
He enters heaven with prayer.

Prayer with our waking thought ascends,
Great God of light, to Thee;
Darkness is banished in the glow
Of Thy reality.

Lo, to our widening vision dawns
The realm of Soul supreme,
Faith-lighted peaks of Spirit stand
Revealed in morning's beam.

Thus in Thy radiance vanishes
Death's drear and gloomy night;
Thus all creation hears anew
Truth's call, Let there be light.

Press on, dear traveler, press thou on,
I am the Way, the Truth, the Life.
It is the straight and narrow way
That leads to that eternal day,
That turns the darkness into light,
That buries wrong and honors right.

Press on, and know that God is all;
He is the Life, the Truth, the Love.
It is the way the Saviour trod,
It is the way that leads to God.
Think of the words: No cross, no crown;
Though tasks are sore, be not cast down.

WILLIAM GASKELL
Adapted

Press on, press on, ye sons of light,
Untiring in your holy fight,
Still treading each temptation down,
And battling for a brighter crown.

Press on, press on, and fear no foe,
With calm resolve to triumph go;
Victorious over every ill,
Press on to higher glory still.

Press on, press on, still look in faith
To Him who conquers sin and death;
Then shall ye hear His word, Well done!
True to the last, press on, press on.

Quiet, Lord, my froward heart,
Make me gentle, pure, and mild,
Upright, simple, free from art;
Make me as a little child,
From distrust and envy free,
Pleased with all that pleaseth Thee.

What Thou shalt today provide
Let me as a child receive,
What tomorrow may betide
Calmly to Thy wisdom leave;
'Tis enough that Thou wilt care,
Why should I the burden bear?

As a little child relies
On a care beyond its own,
Being neither strong nor wise,
Will not take a step alone,
Let me thus with Thee abide,
As my Father, Friend, and Guide.

Put on the whole armor of pure consecration,
The breastplate of righteousness valiantly gird,
With shield of true faith, and the helmet of salvation—
The sword of the Spirit is God's mighty Word!

For His is the greatness, the power and the glory,
The victory His, when for succor we call;
His majesty shines in creation's wondrous story,
And He is exalted as head over all!

Frederic W. Root
Based on hymn by A. M. Toplady

Rock of Ages, Truth divine,
Be Thy strength forever mine;
Let me rest secure on Thee,
Safe above life's raging sea.
Rock of Ages, Truth divine,
Be Thy strength forever mine.

Rock of Truth, our fortress strong,
Thou our refuge from all wrong,
When from mortal sense I flee,
Let me hide myself in Thee.
Rock of Ages, Truth divine,
Be Thy strength forever mine.

Christ, the Truth, foundation sure,
On this rock we are secure;
Peace is there our life to fill,
Cure is there for every ill.
Rock of Ages, Truth divine,
Be Thy strength forever mine.

Based on hymn by M. H. Tipton

Rouse ye, soldiers of the cross,
And lift your banner high;
Servants of a mighty cause,
Put sloth and slumber by.

REFRAIN
Rouse ye, rouse ye, face the foe,
Rise to conquer death and sin;
On with Christ to victory go,
O side with God, and win!

Waken, hear your Captain's call,
And follow where he trod;
Rout the cringing host of fear
By faith that walks with God.

REFRAIN

Rouse ye: long the conquest waits
For valor's act supreme;
Rouse ye, rest not, do the deeds
That break the earthly dream.

REFRAIN

Science, the angel with the flaming sword,
God's gift, the glory of the risen Lord;
Light of the world, in whose light we shall see
Father and perfect Son, blest unity;

Calm of Shekinah where hope anchors fast,
Harbor of refuge till the storm be past;
Sweet, secret place where God and men do meet,
Horeb whereon we walk with unshod feet;

Place of communion with the Lamb of God,
Fold where the sheep must pass beneath His rod;
Ark where the dove may close her faltering wings,
Love's law divine that makes us priests and kings;

Loosener of prison bands at midnight hour,
Of self-forged chains that fall through Love's
all-power;
Christ's morning meal by joyous Galilee:
Science, thou dost fulfill all prophecy.

298
—to—
302

Communion Hymn
Mary Baker Eddy

Saw ye my Saviour? Heard ye the glad sound?
Felt ye the power of the Word?
'Twas the Truth that made us free,
And was found by you and me
In the life and the love of our Lord.

Mourner, it calls you,—"Come to my bosom,
Love wipes your tears all away,
And will lift the shade of gloom,
And for you make radiant room
Midst the glories of one endless day."

Sinner, it calls you,—"Come to this fountain,
Cleanse the foul senses within;
'Tis the Spirit that makes pure,
That exalts thee, and will cure
All thy sorrow and sickness and sin."

Strongest deliverer, friend of the friendless,
Life of all being divine:
Thou the Christ, and not the creed;
Thou the Truth in thought and deed;
Thou the water, the bread, and the wine.

Scorn not the slightest word or deed,
Nor deem it void of power;
There's fruit in each wind-wafted seed
That waits its natal hour.

No act falls fruitless; none can tell
How vast its power may be
Nor what results enfolded dwell
Within it silently.

A whispered word may touch the heart
And call it back to life;
A look of love bid sin depart
And still unholy strife.

Work and despair not; bring thy mite,
Nor care how small it be;
God is with all that serve the right,
The holy, true, and free.

Shepherd, show me how to go
O'er the hillside steep,
How to gather, how to sow,—
How to feed Thy sheep;
I will listen for Thy voice,
Lest my footsteps stray;
I will follow and rejoice
All the rugged way.

Thou wilt bind the stubborn will,
Wound the callous breast,
Make self-righteousness be still,
Break earth's stupid rest.
Strangers on a barren shore,
Lab'ring long and lone,
We would enter by the door,
And Thou know'st Thine own;

So, when day grows dark and cold,
Tear or triumph harms,
Lead Thy lambkins to the fold,
Take them in Thine arms;
Feed the hungry, heal the heart,
Till the morning's beam;
White as wool, ere they depart,
Shepherd, wash them clean.

Sing, ye joyous children, sing,
Glorious is the Christ, our king,
Truth has come again to earth,
Through the lowly Saviour's birth.
Men and angels, anthems raise;
Hymns of joy and shouts of praise.
Hear th' angelic song again:
Peace on earth, good will to men.
Sing, ye joyous children, sing,
Glorious is the Christ, our king.

When the stars together sang,
Then the Truth triumphant rang:
Be there light; And there was light.
Gone are chaos, fear and night;
Truth hath rolled the mists away;
Dawns on earth harmonious day.
Hear th' angelic song again:
Peace on earth, good will to men.
Sing, ye joyous children, sing,
Glorious is the Christ, our king.

So brightly burns Love's holy glow,
So constant shines its light,
That none can claim he doth not know
The pathway through the night,
For see, 'tis lit by Love divine
To trace for us His wise design.

The lambs who wander by the way,
He taketh in His arm;
For in the darkness they did stray
Unconscious of their harm:
So cometh He to all who roam,
To lead them safely, surely home.

To God then praises let us sing
With glad and willing mind
For all the gifts His hand doth bring
To us and all mankind:
Forever doth His gift of love
Pour warmth and radiance from above.

Soldiers of Christ, arise,
And put your armor on,
Strong in the strength which God supplies
Through His eternal Son.
Stand then in His great might,
With all His strength endued,
And take, to arm you for the fight,
The panoply of God.

From strength to strength go on;
O wrestle, fight, and pray;
Tread all the powers of darkness down,
And win the well-fought day.
That, having all things done,
And all your conflicts past,
Ye may o'ercome through Christ alone,
And stand complete at last.

313

William Cowper
Adapted

Sometimes a light surprises
The Christian while he sings;
It is the Lord who rises
With healing in his wings.
When comfort seems declining,
There comes to us again
A season of clear shining,
To cheer us after rain.

In holy contemplation
We sweetly then pursue
The theme of God's salvation,
And find it ever new.
To God, in light abiding,
True praise shall tune my voice,
For while in Him confiding,
I cannot but rejoice.

JAMES MONTGOMERY
Adapted

314

Sow in the morn thy seed,
At eve hold not thy hand;
To doubt and fear give thou no heed;
Broadcast it o'er the land.

It duly shall appear
In verdure, beauty, strength,
The tender blade, the stalk, the ear;
The full corn comes at length.

The harvest now is white;
Lift up thine eyes, behold,
Illumed by Love's transforming light,
God's blessings manifold.

315

316

David Bates

Speak gently, it is better far
To rule by love than fear;
Speak gently, let no harsh word mar
The good we may do here.

Speak gently to the erring ones,
They must have toiled in vain;
Perchance unkindness made them so;
O win them back again.

Speak gently, 'tis a little thing,
Dropped in the heart's deep well;
The good, the joy that it may bring,
Eternity shall tell.

Still, still with Thee when purple morning breaketh,
When the bird waketh, and the shadows flee,
Fairer than morning, lovelier than the daylight,
Dawns the sweet consciousness, I am with Thee.

Alone with Thee, amid the changing shadows,
Solemn the hush of nature, newly born;
Alone with Thee, in breathless adoration,
In the calm dew and freshness of the morn.

So shall it ever be in the bright morning,
When hearts awaking see the shadows flee,
O, in that hour, and fairer than the dawning,
Rises the glorious thought, I am with Thee.

Based on the Danish of
Nikolaj F. S. Grundtvig

Suffer the children to come to me,
This was the Master's tender plea;
Gentle and loving, they are mine,
Ah, will not ye who see this sign
Come unto me?

He who receiveth the Word as they,
Teachable, ready to choose my way,
He shall have peace of sin forgiven,
He shall in this wise enter heaven;
Come unto me.

See ye the lilies, how fair they grow,
Clothed in a glory kings ne'er know;
They, like the sparrows, praise the Lord,
Publish my call with clear accord,
Come unto me.

Sun of our life, thy quickening ray
Sheds on our path the glow of day;
Blest star of hope, thy softened light
Cheers the long watches of the night.

Lord of all life, below, above,
Whose light is truth, whose warmth is love,
Before Thy ever blazing throne
We ask no luster of our own.

Grant us Thy truth to make us free,
And kindling hearts that burn for Thee,
Till all Thy living altars claim
One holy light, one heavenly flame.

320

321

Isaac Watts
Arr. by William Cameron, *Adapted*

Supreme in wisdom as in power,
The Rock of Ages stands;
Canst thou not search His word, and trace
The working of His hands?

He gives the conquest to the meek,
Supports the fainting heart;
And courage in the evil hour
His heavenly aids impart.

Mere human energy shall faint,
And youthful vigor cease;
But those who wait upon the Lord
In strength shall still increase.

They, with unwearied step, shall tread
The path of life divine;
With growing ardor onward move,
With growing brightness shine.

Caroline Gilman
Adapted

Sweet hour of holy, thoughtful prayer,
Thy peace and calm may we improve,
And in God's healing service share
The truths revealed by His dear love.

Lord, may Thy truth upon the heart
Now fall and dwell as heavenly dew,
And flowers of grace in freshness start
Where once the weeds of error grew.

May prayer now lift her sacred wings,
Contented with that aim alone
Which bears her to the King of kings,
And rests her at His sheltering throne.

FRANCES R. HAVERGAL
Adapted

Take my life, and let it be
Consecrated, Lord, to Thee.
Take my moments and my days,
Let them flow in ceaseless praise.
Take my hands, and let them move
At the impulse of Thy love.

Take my feet, and let them be
Swift and beautiful for Thee.
Take my voice, and let me sing
Always, only, for my King.
Take my lips, and let them be
Filled with messages from Thee.

Take my every thought, to use
In the way that Thou shalt choose.
Take my love; O Lord, I pour
At Thy feet its treasure store.
I am Thine, and I will be
Ever, only, all for Thee.

Charles W. Everest
Adapted

Take up thy cross, the Saviour said,
If thou wouldst my disciple be;
Thyself deny, the world forsake,
And humbly follow after me.

Take up thy cross, nor heed the shame;
Let not thy foolish pride rebel;
Thy Lord for thee the cross endured,
He conquered sin, and death, and hell.

Take up thy cross, in God's own strength,
Calmly all fear and danger brave;
So shalt thou find immortal Life
Giveth thee victory o'er the grave.

The Christian warrior, see him stand
In all the armor of his God;
The Spirit's sword is in his hand;
His feet are with the gospel shod:

In panoply of truth complete,
Salvation's helmet on his head,
With righteousness, a breastplate meet,
And faith's broad shield before him spread.

With this omnipotence he moves;
From this the alien armies flee;
Until he more than conqueror proves,
Through Christ, who gives him victory.

Thus strong in his Redeemer's strength,
Sin, death and hell he tramples down,
Fights his good fight and wins at length,
Through mercy, an immortal crown.

The God who made both heaven and earth
And all that they contain
Will never quit His steadfast truth
Nor make His promise vain.

The poor and all oppressed by wrong
Are saved by His decree;
He gives the hungry needful food
And sets the captive free.

By Him the blind receive their sight,
By Him the fallen rise;
With constant care, His tender love
All human need supplies.

The heavens declare the glory
Of Him who made all things;
Each day repeats the story,
Each night its tribute brings.
To earth's remotest border
His mighty power is known;
In beauty, grandeur, order,
His handiwork is shown.

His law man's pathway brightens,
His judgments all are pure,
His Word the thought enlightens,
And ever shall endure.
To heed His testimony,
And Wisdom's way to hold,
Is sweeter far than honey,
And better far than gold.

In daily contemplation
Of Thee, I take delight;
O, let my meditation
Lay hold of Thee aright.
O, aid me in suppression
Of idle thought or word;
O, keep me from transgression,
Redeemer, strength, and Lord.

The King of Love my Shepherd is,
Whose goodness faileth never;
I nothing lack, for I am His
And He is mine forever.

Where streams of living water flow
My ransomed soul He leadeth,
And where the verdant pastures grow,
With food celestial feedeth.

Perverse and foolish oft I strayed,
But yet in love He sought me,
And on His shoulder gently laid,
And home, rejoicing, brought me.

And so through all the length of days
Thy goodness faileth never;
Good Shepherd, may I sing Thy praise
Within Thy house forever.

The lifted eye and bended knee
Are but vain homage, Lord, to Thee;
In vain our lips Thy praise prolong,
The heart a stranger to the song.

The pure, the humble, contrite mind,
Sincere and to Thy will resigned,
To Thee a nobler offering yields
Than Sheba's groves or Sharon's fields.

Love God and man: this great command
Doth on eternal pillars stand;
This did Thine ancient prophets teach,
And this Thy Well-Beloved preach.

Based on the Danish of
NIKOLAJ F. S. GRUNDTVIG

The Lord is in His holy place,
Let all the earth be still,
Be still and know that He is God,
And wait to do His will.
We need a sacred watchfulness,
An earnest deep desire for grace,
Our lives with true content to fill.

So hear and heed His faithful Word,
And trust His promise long,
For they who seek Him Life shall find,
And shall in Him be strong;
We need a perfect faith in Him,
With understanding never dim,
To fill our daily lives with song.

The loving friend to all who bowed
Beneath life's weary load,
From lips baptized in humble prayer,
His consolations flowed.

The faithful witness to the truth,
His just rebuke was hurled
Out from a heart that burned to break
The fetters of the world.

No hollow rite, no lifeless creed,
His piercing glance could bear;
But longing hearts which sought him found
That God and heaven were there.

The spirit breathes upon the Word
And brings the truth to sight;
Precept and promise still afford
A sanctifying light.

A glory gilds the sacred page,
Majestic like the sun;
It gives a light to every age,
It gives but borrows none.

Let everlasting thanks be Thine
For such a bright display
As makes a world of darkness shine
With beams of heavenly day.

The morning light is breaking,
The darkness disappears;
The sons of earth are waking
To penitential tears.
Each breeze that sweeps the ocean
Brings tidings from afar,
Of nations in commotion,
Prepared for Zion’s war.

Blest river of salvation,
Pursue thine onward way;
Flow thou to every nation,
Nor in thy richness stay:
Stay not till all the lowly
Triumphant reach their home:
Stay not till all the holy
Proclaim, The Lord is come.

The starry firmament on high,
And all the glories of the sky,
These shine not to Thy praise, O Lord,
So brightly as Thy sacred Word.

The hope Thy holy Word supplies,
Its truth divine and precepts wise,
In each a heavenly beam I see,
And every beam conducts to Thee.

And fixed for everlasting years,
Unmoved, amid dissolving spheres,
Thy Word shall shine in cloudless day,
When heaven and earth have past away.

Theories, which thousands cherish,
Pass like clouds that sweep the sky;
Creeds and dogmas all may perish;
Truth Herself can never die.

Worldlings blindly may refuse Her,
Close their eyes and call it night;
Learned scoffers may abuse Her,
But they cannot quench Her light.

Thrones may totter, empires crumble,
All their glories cease to be;
While She, Christlike, crowns the humble,
And from bondage sets them free.

There are none friendless, none afraid,
The saving Truth who know,
Their shining path leads from the shade,
And up to light they go.

It setteth free from thought of sin,
It healeth sorrow's blight,
Immortal joy is found therein,
And there shall be no night.

And O, may we, God's children true,
His healing love make known,
And see by faith all things made new
When ruled by Love alone.

There's a wideness in God's mercy,
Like the wideness of the sea;
There's a kindness in His justice,
Which is more than liberty.

For the love of God is broader
Than is seen by human mind,
And the heart of the Eternal
Is most wonderfully kind.

If our love were but more simple,
We should take Him at His word;
And our lives would be all sunshine
In the sweetness of our Lord.

They who seek the throne of grace,
Find that throne in every place:
If we live a life of prayer,
God is present everywhere.

In our sickness, in our health,
In our want, or in our wealth,
If we look to God in prayer,
God is present everywhere.

Then, my heart, in every strait,
To thy Father come, and wait;
He will answer every prayer,
God is present everywhere.

This is the day the Lord hath made;
Be glad, give thanks, rejoice;
Stand in His presence, unafraid,
In praise lift up your voice.
All perfect gifts are from above,
And all our blessings show
The amplitude of God's dear love
Which every heart may know.

The Lord will hear before we call,
And every need supply;
Good things are freely given to all
Who on His word rely.
We come today to bring Him praise
Not for such gifts alone,
But for the higher, deeper ways
In which His love is shown.

For sin destroyed, for sorrow healed,
For health and peace restored;
For Life and Love by Truth revealed,
We thank and bless the Lord.
This is the day the Lord hath made,
In praise lift up your voice.
In shining robes of joy arrayed,
Be glad, give thanks, rejoice.

George W. Doane
Adapted

Thou art the Way: to thee alone
From sin and death we flee;
And he who would the Father seek,
Must seek Him, Lord, by thee.

Thou art the Truth: thy word alone
True wisdom doth impart;
Thou only canst unfold that Truth,
And purify the heart.

Thou art the Life: the rending tomb
Proclaims thy conquering arm;
And those who put their trust in thee
Nor death nor hell shall harm.

Thou art the Way, the Truth, the Life:
Grant us that Way to know,
That Truth to trust, that Life to learn,
Whose joys eternal flow.

Thou living light of pentecostal glory,
Lo, wide we fling the sunless prison doors;
Thy cleansing fire repeats its ancient story
To purge and hallow us, the splendor pours.

Perfect and pure, ineffable in beauty,
Thy stainless radiance e'en to us impart,
Till in reflection finding all our duty,
We see the glory shine from heart to heart.

So all shall see where Thine effulgence gloweth,
Through purer lives of men, a countless host,
So all shall learn how God Himself bestoweth
His priceless pearl of gifts, the Holy Ghost.

Thou whose almighty Word
Chaos and darkness heard,
And took their flight;
Hear us, we humbly pray,
And where the Gospel-day
Sheds not its glorious ray,
Let there be light.

Christ, thou dost come to bring
On thy redeeming wing
Healing and sight,
Health to the sick in mind,
Sight to the inly blind;
Ah, now to all mankind
Let there be light.

Spirit of truth and love,
Life-giving, holy dove,
Speed forth thy flight;
Move on the waters' face,
Bearing the lamp of grace,
And in earth's darkest place
Let there be light.

Though mountains may depart from thee,
And hills be far removed,
His kindness shall remain with thee,
His covenant be proved.

O thou afflicted, tossed with doubt,
God bids the storm to cease;
His children shall be taught of Him
And great shall be their peace.

Established in His righteousness,
He holds thee free from fear;
No weapon formed against His own
Shall prosper nor come near.

All tongues that rise condemning thee
Are silenced by His word;
This is thy precious heritage,
Thou servant of the Lord.

Thy will, almighty Father, Thine,
And Thine alone be ever done;
For Thou art Life and Truth and Love,
The great, eternal, Holy One.

Reflecting truly all Thou art
And all the sunshine of Thy love,
No life we know from Thee apart,
But peace on earth from heaven above.

We walk in freedom and in peace
Thy holy purpose to fulfill,
And Thou dost ever point the path
For loving servants of Thy will.

350

Mary Peters
Adapted

Through the love of God our Saviour
All will be well;
Free and changeless is His favor;
All must be well;
Precious is the love that healed us,
Perfect is the grace that sealed us,
Strong the hand stretched forth to shield us;
All, all is well.

Though we pass through tribulation,
All will be well;
Ours is such a full salvation,
All must be well;
Happy still, in God confiding,
Fruitful, when in Christ abiding,
Holy, through the Spirit's guiding;
All, all is well.

We expect a bright tomorrow,
All will be well;
Faith can sing through days of sorrow,
All must be well;
While His truth we are applying,
And upon His love relying,
God is every need supplying,
All, all is well.

BERNHARD S. INGEMANN
S. BARING-GOULD, TR.

Through the night of doubt and sorrow
Onward goes the pilgrim band,
Singing songs of expectation,
Marching to the promised land.
Clear before us through the darkness
Gleams and burns the guiding light;
Brother clasps the hand of brother,
Stepping fearless through the night.

One, the light of God's own presence,
O'er His ransomed people shed,
Chasing far the gloom and terror,
Brightening all the path we tread:
One, the object of our journey,
One, the faith which never tires,
One, the earnest looking forward,
One, the hope our God inspires;

One, the strain the lips of thousands
Lift as from the heart of one;
One the conflict, one the peril,
One, the march in God begun:
One, the gladness of rejoicing
On the far eternal shore
Where the One Almighty Father
Reigns in love forevermore.

352
—
353

ARTHUR C. COXE
Adapted

Thy works, how beauteous, how divine,
That in true meekness used to shine,
That lit thy lonely pathway, trod
In wondrous love, O Son of God.

O, who like thee so calm, so bright,
So pure, so made to live in light?
O, who like thee did ever go
So patient through a world of woe?

O, who like thee so humbly bore
Scorn and the scoffs of men, before?
So meek, forgiving, Godlike, high,
So glorious in humility.

O, in thy light be mine to go,
Let it illume my way of woe
And give me ever on the road
To trace thy footsteps, Son of God.

BENJAMIN BEDDOME
Adapted

'Tis God the Spirit leads
In paths before unknown;
The work to be performed is ours,
The strength is all His own.

Supported by His grace,
We still pursue our way;
Assured that we shall reach the prize,
Secure in endless day.

God works in us to will,
He works in us to do;
His is the power by which we act,
His be the glory too.

Truth comes alike to all
Who on Her name dare call
With motives pure;
Then let us all unite,
With freedom's star in sight,
Press onward in the right,
Which shall endure.

Come, all pervading Love,
Thou heart of heaven above,
O Spirit blest.
Life, Truth and Love shall be
Our glorious trinity,
And every heart shall see
Eternal rest.

To Thee, O God, we bring our adoration,
To Love divine, in whom we live and move;
For Thou hast shown to us our perfect selfhood
In Thy loved Son, whom Jesus came to prove.

We are Thy children, Thou our Father-Mother,
And we would ever follow Thy behest:
Help us to understand Thy holy counsel,
For in obedience lies our active rest.

We, now redeemed through Love, return to Zion,
Singing to Thee our deeply grateful praise;
For we are Christ's, and Christ is Thine, O Father:
His joy remains in us through endless days.

To Thee, our loving Father, God,
A gladsome song begin,
Whose smile is on the world abroad,
Whose joy our hearts within.

We need not, Lord, our gladness leave,
To worship Thee aright;
Our joyfulness for praise receive,
Thou mak'st our lives so bright.

The pure in heart are always glad;
The smile of God they feel;
He doth the secret of His joy
To blameless hearts reveal.

Trust the Eternal when the shadows gather,
When joys of daylight seem so like a dream;
God the unchanging pities like a father;
Trust on and wait, the daystar yet shall gleam.

Trust the Eternal, for the clouds that vanish
No more can move the mountains from their base
Than sin's illusive wreaths of mist can banish
Light from His throne or loving from His face.

Trust the Eternal, and repent in meekness
Of that heart's pride which frowns and will not yield,
Then to thy child-heart shall come strength in weakness,
And thine immortal life shall be revealed.

Elizabeth Charles
Adapted

True, the heart grows rich in giving;
All its wealth is living grain;
Seeds which mildew in the garner,
Scattered, fill with gold the plain.
Is thy burden hard and heavy?
Do thy steps drag wearily?
Help to bear thy brother's burden,
God will bear both it and thee.

Is the heart a well left empty?
None but God its void can fill;
Nothing but a ceaseless fountain
Can its ceaseless longings still.
Is the heart a living power?
Self-entwined its strength sinks low;
It can only live in loving,
And, by serving, love will grow.

Paul Gerhardt
Based on Danish translation of Stener J. Stenersen

Trust all to God, the Father,
Confide thou in none other,
He is thy sole defense;
He cares for thee past measure,
Seek Him who has thy treasure,
Thy helper is omnipotence.

Behold His works of wonder,
Yea, all His doings ponder,
Else is thy toil in vain;
Thy caring and contriving,
Thy taking thought and striving
Are naught unless the Lord ordain.

God lights the way of duty,
And gives, for ashes, beauty,
And naught His hand delays;
Who trusts in His providing,
All glad in this confiding,
Is he who without ceasing prays.

362

JOHN MORISON
Adapted

To us a Child of Hope is born,
To us a Son is given;
Him shall the tribes of earth obey,
And all the hosts of heaven.

His name shall be the Prince of Peace,
Forevermore adored;
The Wonderful, the Counsellor,
The great and mighty Lord.

His power, increasing, still shall spread;
His reign shall never cease;
For justice ever guards his throne,
And all his paths are peace.

John Bowring
Adapted

Upon the Gospel's sacred page
The gathered beams of ages shine;
And, as it hastens, every age
But makes its brightness more divine.

On mightier wing, in loftier flight,
From year to year does knowledge soar;
And, as it soars, the Gospel light
Becomes effulgent more and more.

More glorious still, as centuries roll,
New regions blest, new powers unfurled,
So Truth reveals the perfect whole,
Its radiance shall o'erflow the world,—

Shall flow to bless but not destroy;
As when the cloudless lamp of day
Pours out its floods of light and joy,
And sweeps the lingering mist away.

Harriet Auber
Adapted

Vainly, through night's weary hours,
Keep we watch, lest foes alarm;
Vain our bulwarks and our towers,
But for God's protecting arm.

Vain were all our toil and labor,
Did not God that labor bless;
Vain, without His grace and favor,
Every talent we possess.

Vainer still the hope of heaven
That on human strength relies;
But to him all good is given
Who in faith to God applies.

Wait, my soul, upon the Lord,
To His gracious promise flee,
Laying hold upon His Word:
As thy days thy strength shall be.

If the sorrows of thy case
Seem peculiar still to thee,
God has promised needful grace:
As thy days thy strength shall be.

Rock of Ages, I'm secure
With Thy promise full and free,
Faithful, positive, and sure:
As thy days thy strength shall be.

Walk in the light, so thou shalt know
That fellowship of love
His spirit only can bestow
Who reigns in light above.

Walk in the light, and thou shalt find
Thy heart made truly His,
Who dwells in cloudless light enshrined,
In whom no darkness is.

Walk in the light, and thou shalt own
Thy darkness past away,
Because that light on thee hath shone
In which is perfect day.

Walk in the light, and thou shalt see
Thy path, though thorny, bright;
For God by grace shall dwell with thee,
And God Himself is Light.

Watchman, tell us of the night,
What its signs of promise are;
Traveler, o'er yon mountain's height
See that glory-beaming star;
Watchman, does its beauteous ray
Aught of hope or joy foretell?
Traveler, yes; it brings the day,
Promised day of Israel.

Watchman, tell us of the night,
Higher yet that star ascends;
Traveler, blessedness and light,
Peace and truth its course portends;
Watchman, will its beams alone
Gild the spot that gave them birth?
Traveler, ages are its own;
See, it bursts o'er all the earth.

Watchman, tell us of the night,
For the morning seems to dawn;
Traveler, darkness takes its flight,
Doubt and terror are withdrawn;
Watchman, let thy wanderings cease,
Hie thee to thy quiet home.
Traveler, lo, the Prince of Peace,
Lo, the Son of God is come.

We are hid with Christ forever
In the Father's holy plan.
In this pure eternal union
We behold the perfect man;
And we know that sin can never
Overthrow the sacred rod
Of dominion over evil:
We are hid with Christ in God.

Hid with Christ in God, O gladness:
O the meekness and the might,
When the risen Christ has lifted
All our thoughts into the light,
Light of Truth wherein no sadness
Dims the radiant peace we find,
As we set our whole affection
On the beauteous things of Mind.

We lift our hearts in praise,
O God of Life, to Thee,
And would reflect in all our ways
Thy purity.
Thy thoughts our lives enfold,
And free us from all fear;
All strife is stilled, all grief consoled,
For Thou art here.

We lift our hearts in praise,
O God of Truth, to Thee,
And find within Thy perfect law
Our liberty.
We bless Thy mighty name
In this exalted hour,
And to the world in faith proclaim
Thy healing power.

We lift our hearts in praise,
O God of Love, to Thee,
With joy to find through darkened days
Thy harmony.
O Father-Mother Love,
We triumph 'neath Thy rod,
We glory in Thy light, and prove
That Thou art God.

We may not climb the heavenly steeps
To bring the Lord Christ down;
In vain we search the lowest deeps,
For him no depths can drown:

But warm, sweet, tender, even yet
A present help is he;
And faith has yet its Olivet,
And love its Galilee.

The healing of the seamless dress
Is by our beds of pain;
We touch him in life's throng and press,
And we are whole again.

O Lord and Master of us all,
Whate'er our name or sign,
We own thy sway, we hear thy call,
We test our lives by thine.

We thank Thee and we bless Thee,
O Father of us all,
That e'en before we ask Thee
Thou hear'st Thy children's call.
We praise Thee for Thy goodness
And tender, constant care,
We thank Thee, Father-Mother,
That Thou hast heard our prayer.

We thank Thee and we bless Thee,
O Lord of all above,
That now Thy children know Thee
As everlasting Love.
And Love is not the author
Of discord, pain and fear;
O Love divine, we thank Thee
That good alone is here.

We thank Thee, Father-Mother,
For blessings, light and grace
Which bid mankind to waken
And see Thee face to face.
We thank Thee, when in anguish
We turn from sense to Soul
That we may hear Thee calling:
Rejoice, for thou art whole.

We thank Thee, heavenly Father,
For Thy correcting rod,
Which guides us in our journey
And leads us home to God.
It tells us not of anger,
The weapon mortals sway,
But Love divine, that helps us
To keep the better way.

O may we tread the pathway,
Nor ever turn aside,
Allured by ways of error,
Whose paths are broad and wide.
Toward Thee, while pressing onward,
The way will brighter grow,
For Thou throughout the journey
Thy loving care wilt show.

We turn to Thee, O Lord,
And sing in sweet accord;
We would Thy beauty see,
Lifting our lives to Thee,
Thou art God.

Our hearts redeemed from strife,
And comforted in grief,
Healing and joy are ours,
Blessings of peaceful hours,
Thou art Life.

O God, we bless Thy name,
Thy wondrous power acclaim,
Lord, Thy salvation strong,
Now is become our song,
Great I AM.

379
380

CATHERINE WINKWORTH, TR.*
From the German

Well for him who, all things losing,
E'en himself doth count as naught,
Still the one thing needful choosing
That with all true bliss is fraught.

Well for him who nothing knoweth
But his God, whose boundless love
Makes the heart wherein it gloweth
Calm and pure and faithful prove.

Well for him who, all forsaking,
Walketh not in shadows vain,
But the path of peace is taking
Through the vale of tears and pain.

O that we our hearts might sever
From earth's tempting vanities,
Fixing them on Him forever
In whom all our fullness lies.

What brightness dawned in resurrection
And shone in Mary's wondering eyes!
Her heart was thrilled with new affection,
She saw her Lord in life arise.

She knew the Christ, undimmed by dying,
Alive forevermore to save;
Creative Mind, all good supplying,
Had triumphed over cross and grave.

With hope and faith, like exiles yearning
For homelands loved through patient years,
The hearts of men are homeward turning
To God Who giveth rest from fears.

Assured and safe in Love's protection,
Great peace have they, and unsought joy;
They rise from sin in resurrection,
And works of love their hands employ.

What is thy birthright, man,
Child of the perfect One;
What is thy Father's plan
For His beloved son?

Thou art Truth's honest child,
Of pure and sinless heart;
Thou treadest undefiled
In Christly paths apart.

Vain dreams shall disappear
As Truth dawns on the sight;
The phantoms of thy fear
Shall flee before the light.

Take then the sacred rod;
Thou art not error's thrall;
Thou hast the gift of God—
Dominion over all.

Whatever dims thy sense of truth
Or stains thy purity,
Though light as breath of summer air,
O count it sin to thee.

Preserve the tablet of thy thoughts
From every blemish free.
For our Redeemer's holy faith
Its temple makes with thee.

And pray of God, that grace be given
To tread the narrow way:
How dark soever it may seem,
It leads to cloudless day.

HOSEA BALLOU
Adapted

When God is seen with men to dwell,
And all creation makes anew,
What tongue can half the wonders tell,
What eye the dazzling glories view?

Celestial streams shall gently flow,
The wilderness shall joyful be;
On parched ground shall lilies grow
And gladness spring on every tree;

The weak be strong, the fearful bold,
The deaf shall hear, the dumb shall sing,
The lame shall walk, the blind behold,
And joy through all the earth shall ring.

When Israel, of the Lord beloved,
Out of the land of bondage came,
Her fathers' God before her moved,
An awful guide, in smoke and flame.

And present still, though oft unseen
When brightly shines the prosperous day,
Be thoughts of Thee a cloudy screen
To temper the deceitful ray.

And O, when stoops on Judah's path
In shade and storm the frequent night,
Be Thou, long-suffering, slow to wrath,
A burning and a shining light.

386
387

ISAAC WATTS
Adapted

When Jesus our great Master came
To teach us in his Father's name,
In every act, in every thought,
He lived the precepts which he taught.

So let our lips and lives express
The holy gospel we profess;
So let our works and virtues shine,
To prove the doctrine all divine.

Thus shall we best proclaim abroad,
The honors of our Saviour, God,
When His salvation reigns within,
And grace subdues the claim of sin.

JAMES MONTGOMERY
Adapted

When like a stranger on our sphere
The lowly Jesus sojourned here,
Where'er he went affliction fled,
The sick were healed, the hungry fed.

With bounding steps the halt and lame
To hail their great deliverer came;
For him the grave could hold no dread,
He spoke the word and raised the dead.

Through paths of loving-kindness led,
Where Jesus triumphed we would tread;
To all with willing hands dispense
The gifts of our benevolence.

While Thou, O my God, art my help and defender,
No cares can o'erwhelm me, no terrors appall;
The wiles and the snares of this world will but render
More lively my hope in my God and my all.

Yes, Thou art my refuge in sorrow and danger;
My strength, should I suffer; my hope, should I fall;
My comfort and joy in this land of the stranger;
My treasure, my glory, my God, and my all.

WILLIAM F. SHERWIN
Adapted

390

Why is thy faith in God's great love so small?
Why doth thy heart shrink back at duty's call?
Art thou obeying this: Abide in me;
And doth the Master's word abide in thee?

O blest assurance from our risen Lord;
O precious comfort breathing from the Word.
How great the promise, could there greater be?
Ask what thou wilt, it shall be done for thee.

Ask what thou wilt, but O, remember this,
We ask and have not when we ask amiss.
If weak in faith, we only half believe
That what we ask we really shall receive.

Why search the future and the past?
Why do ye look with tearful eyes
And seek far off for paradise?
Before your feet Life's pearl is cast.

As deathless as His spirit free,
The Perfect lives and works today
As in the ancient prophets' lay,
Where there's an open eye to see.

Of all that was and is to come
The present holds the Mind and Cause;
For God lives in eternal laws,
And here today upholds His throne.

Then rise and greet the signs that prove
Unreal the ages' long lament;
The "one far-off divine event"
Is now, and that event is Love.

With love and peace and joy supreme
We hail the new appearing;
From out the darkness and the dream,
The haven of rest is nearing.

With gifts of healing in his wings
To light the Christ now guides us,
The heart that knows him burns and sings,
For endless joy betides us.

His touch the door of Life unseals
And bids us freely enter,
His word the heaven of heavens reveals
With Love its bound and center.

For God is all, and Christ the way;
Our meek and bold defender
Has cleft the night and lo, the day
Bursts forth in mighty splendor.

394
—
395

Jonathan F. Bahnmaier
Tr. Catherie Winkworth

Word of Life, most pure, most strong,
Lo, for thee the nations long;
Spread, till from its dreary night
All the world awakes to light.

Lo, the ripening fields we see,
Mighty shall the harvest be;
But the reapers still are few,
Great the work they have to do.

Lord of harvest, let there be
Joy and strength to work for Thee,
Till the nations far and near
See Thy light, Thy law revere.

Mrs. Vokes
Adapted

Ye messengers of Christ,
His sovereign voice obey;
Arise, and follow where he leads,
And peace attend your way.

The Master whom you serve
Will needful strength bestow;
Depending on his promised aid,
With sacred courage go.

In vain shall evil strive,
And hell in vain oppose;
The cause is God's and will prevail,
In spite of all His foes.

398

Philip Doddridge
Adapted

Ye servants of the Lord,
Each in his office wait,
Observant of His heavenly word,
And watchful at His gate.

Let all your lamps be bright,
The golden flame burn clear;
The signal cometh through the night;
The bridegroom draweth near.

O, happy servant he,
In watchful service found;
He shall his Lord with rapture see,
And be with honor crowned.

WILLIAM COWPER
Adapted

Ye timid saints, fresh courage take,
The clouds ye so much dread
Are big with mercy, and will break
In blessings on your head.

His mighty purpose ripens fast,
Unfolding every hour;
The bud may have a bitter taste,
But sweet will be the flower.

Blind unbelief is sure to err,
And scan His work in vain;
God is His own interpreter,
And He will make it plain.

Thou whose almighty Word
Chaos and darkness heard,
And took their flight;
Hear us, we humbly pray,
And where the Gospel-day
Sheds not its glorious ray,
Let there be light.

Christ, thou dost come to bring
On thy redeeming wing
Healing and sight,
Health to the sick in mind,
Sight to the inly blind;
Ah, now to all mankind
Let there be light.

Spirit of truth and love,
Life-giving, holy dove,
Speed forth thy flight;
Move on the waters' face,
Bearing the lamp of grace,
And in earth's darkest place
Let there be light.

PHILIP DODDRIDGE
Adapted

How gentle God's commands,
How kind His precepts are;
Come, cast your burdens on the Lord,
And trust His constant care.

Beneath His watchful eye
His saints securely dwell;
That hand which bears creation up
Shall guard His children well.

His goodness stands approved,
Unchanged from day to day:
I drop my burden at His feet,
And bear a song away.

403

Joseph Swain
Adapted

How sweet, how heavenly is the sight,
When those who love the Lord
In one another's peace delight,
And so fulfill His word;

When, free from envy, scorn, and pride,
Our wishes all above,
Each can his brother's failings hide,
And show a brother's love.

Let love, in one delightful stream,
Through every bosom flow;
And union sweet, and dear esteem
In every action glow.

Love is the golden chain that binds
The hearts that faithful prove;
And he's an heir of heaven who finds
His bosom glow with love.

O do not bar your mind
Against the light of good;
But open wide, let in the Word,
And Truth will be your food.

Truth will from error free
Your long enslaved mind,
And bring the light of liberty
Where it shall be enshrined.

Hid treasures it reveals
To all who know its power;
And all who will may light receive
In this most gracious hour.

Then open wide your heart
To Truth and Light and Love;
You then shall know your life is hid
With Christ in God above.

CHARLES WESLEY AND JOHN TAYLOR
Adapted

Glory be to God on high,
God whose glory fills the sky;
Peace on earth to man is given,
Man, the well-beloved of heaven.
Gracious Father, in Thy love,
Send Thy blessings from above;
Let Thy light, Thy truth, Thy peace
Bid all strife and tumult cease.

Mark the wonders of His hand:
Power no empire can withstand;
Wisdom, angels' glorious theme;
Goodness one eternal stream.
All ye people, raise the song,
Endless thanks to God belong;
Hearts o'erflowing with His praise
Join the hymns your voices raise.

O Love, our Mother, ever near,
To Thee we turn from doubt and fear!
In perfect peace our thoughts abide;
Our hearts now in this truth confide:
Man is the child of God.

O Light, in Thy light we can see
That man is ever one with Thee.
In love our lives Thou dost enfold,
And now our waiting hopes behold
That man is God's own child.

O joy that ever will remain,
Midst seeming sorrow, hate, and pain,
Our hearts to fill with this glad song
That soars above the mists of wrong:
Man is the loved of Love.

To Thee, our loving Father, God,
A gladsome song begin,
Whose smile is on the world abroad,
Whose joy our hearts within.

We need not, Lord, our gladness leave,
To worship Thee aright;
Our joyfulness for praise receive,
Thou mak'st our lives so bright.

The pure in heart are always glad;
The smile of God they feel;
He doth the secret of His joy
To blameless hearts reveal.

Prayer with our waking thought ascends,
Great God of light, to Thee;
Darkness is banished in the glow
Of Thy reality.

Lo, to our widening vision dawns
The realm of Soul supreme,
Faith-lighted peaks of Spirit stand
Revealed in morning's beam.

Thus in Thy radiance vanishes
Death's drear and gloomy night;
Thus all creation hears anew
Truth's call, Let there be light.

409

Isaac Watts
Arr. by William Cameron, *Adapted*

Supreme in wisdom as in power,
The Rock of Ages stands;
Canst thou not search His word, and trace
The working of His hands?

He gives the conquest to the meek,
Supports the fainting heart;
And courage in the evil hour
His heavenly aids impart.

Mere human energy shall faint,
And youthful vigor cease;
But those who wait upon the Lord
In strength shall still increase.

They, with unwearied step, shall tread
The path of life divine;
With growing ardor onward move,
With growing brightness shine.

No mortal sense can still or stay
The flight of silent prayer,
Unceasing, voiceless, heart desire
That seeks God everywhere.

The heart's own longing lifts it high
Where words can never reach,
Though human lips may never form
That glory into speech.

The voices that are worldly wise,
With mortal modes in tune,
Are mute in that transcendent hour
When God and man commune.

411

Frederic W. Root
Based on hymn by Martin Luther

All power is given unto our Lord,
On Him we place reliance;
With truth from out His sacred word
We bid our foes defiance.
With Him we shall prevail,
Whatever may assail;
He is our shield and tower,
Almighty is His power;
His kingdom is forever.

Rejoice, ye people, praise His name,
His care doth e'er surround us.
His love to error's thralldom came,
And from its chains unbound us.
Our Lord is God alone,
No other power we own;
No other voice we heed,
No other help we need;
His kingdom is forever.

O then give thanks to God on high,
Who life to all is giving;
The hosts of death before Him fly,
In Him we all are living.
Then let us know no fear,
Our King is ever near;
Our stay and fortress strong,
Our strength, our hope, our song;
His kingdom is forever.

O dreamer, leave thy dreams for joyful waking,
O captive, rise and sing, for thou art free;
The Christ is here, all dreams of error breaking,
Unloosing bonds of all captivity.

He comes to bless thee on his wings of healing;
To banish pain, and wipe all tears away;
He comes anew, to humble hearts revealing
The mounting footsteps of the upward way.

He comes to give thee joy for desolation,
Beauty for ashes of the vanished years;
For every tear to bring full compensation,
To give thee confidence for all thy fears.

He comes to call the dumb to joyful singing;
The deaf to hear; the blinded eyes to see;
The glorious tidings of salvation bringing.
O captive, rise, thy Saviour comes to thee.

Let us sing of Easter gladness
That rejoices every day,
Sing of hope and faith uplifted;
Love has rolled the stone away.
Lo, the promise and fulfillment,
Lo, the man whom God hath made,
Seen in glory of an Easter
Crowned with light that cannot fade.

When we touch Truth's healing garment
And behold Life's purity,
When we find in Love the refuge
That is man's security,
When we turn from earth to Spirit,
And from self have won release,
Then we see the risen Saviour;
Then we know his promised peace.

Living meekly as the Master,
Who of God was glorified,
Looking ever to the radiance
Of his wondrous Eastertide;
Freed of fear, of pain, and sorrow,
Giving God the honor due,
Every day will be an Easter
Filled with benedictions new.

I love to tell the story
Of unseen things above,
Of Jesus and his glory,
Of Jesus and his love,
I love to tell the story
Because I know 'tis true,
It satisfies my longing
As nothing else can do.

REFRAIN

I love to tell the story,
It is my theme in glory
To tell the old, old story
Of Jesus and his love.

I love to tell the story,
'Tis pleasant to repeat
What seems, each time I tell it,
More wonderfully sweet.
I love to tell the story,
For some have never heard
The message of salvation
From God's own holy word.

REFRAIN

— *continued on next page* —

414
continued

I love to tell the story,
For those who know it best
Seem hungering and thirsting
To hear it like the rest,
I love to tell the story,
To sing the new, new song
That is the old, old story,
That I have loved so long.

REFRAIN

I'm a pilgrim, and I'm a stranger;
I can tarry, I can tarry but a night.
Do not detain me, for I am going
To where the fountains are ever flowing:

REFRAIN

I'm a pilgrim, and I'm a stranger;
I can tarry, I can tarry but a night.

There the glory is ever shining;
O, my longing heart, my longing heart is there.
Here in this country so dark and dreary,
I long have wandered forlorn and weary:

REFRAIN

There's the city to which I journey;
My Redeemer, my Redeemer, is its light.
There is no sorrow, nor any sighing,
Nor any tears there, nor any dying:

REFRAIN

KATE L. COLBY
Adapted

Be true and list the voice within,
Be true unto thy high ideal,
Thy perfect self, that knows no sin,
That self that is the only real.

God is the only perfect One:
My perfect self is one with Him;
So man is seen as God's own son,
When Truth dispels the shadows dim.

True to our God whose name is Love,
We shall fulfill our Father's plan;
For true means true to God above,
To self, and to our fellow man.

Isaac Watts
Adapted

Joy to the world, the Lord is come,
Let earth receive her King;
Let every heart prepare him room,
And heaven and nature sing.

No more let sin and sorrow grow,
Nor thorns infest the ground;
Where'er he comes, his blessings flow,
And hope and joy abound.

He rules the world with truth and grace,
And makes the nations prove
The glories of his righteousness
And wonders of his love.

O, the clanging bells of time,
Night and day they never cease;
We are wearied with their chime,
For they do not bring us peace;
And we hush our breath to hear,
And we strain our eyes to see
If thy shores are drawing near,
Eternity! Eternity!

O, the clanging bells of time,
How their changes rise and fall,
But in undertone sublime,
Sounding clearly through them all,
Is a voice that must be heard,
As our moments onward flee,
And it speaketh, aye, one word,
Eternity! Eternity!

O, the clanging bells of time,
To their voices, loud and low,
In a long, unresting line
We are marching to and fro;
And we yearn for sight or sound
Of the life that is to be,
For thy breath doth wrap us round,
Eternity! Eternity!

— continued on next page —

O, the clanging bells of time,
Soon their notes will all be dumb,
And in joy and peace sublime,
We shall feel the silence come;
And our souls their thirst will slake,
And our eyes the King will see,
When thy glorious morn shall break,
Eternity! Eternity!

O Love whose perfect path is known
To all who walk the ways of God,
Whose mysteries are so clearly shown
To pilgrims with the gospel shod;

Thy radiance is so pure, so free,
So beautiful and swift to bless,
That by reflection constantly
We manifest Thy tenderness:

And every sacred shrine shall burn
With flames of Truth divinely bright,
And every weary child shall turn
In gratitude toward Thee, the Light.

So brightly burns Love's holy glow,
So constant shines its light,
That none can claim he doth not know
The pathway through the night,
For see, 'tis lit by Love divine
To trace for us His wise design.

The lambs who wander by the way,
He taketh in His arm;
For in the darkness they did stray
Unconscious of their harm:
So cometh He to all who roam,
To lead them safely, surely home.

To God then praises let us sing
With glad and willing mind
For all the gifts His hand doth bring
To us and all mankind:
Forever doth His gift of love
Pour warmth and radiance from above.

From these Thy children gathered in Thy name,
From hearts made whole, from lips redeemed
from woe,
Thy praise, O Father, shall forever flow.
Alleluia! Alleluia!

O perfect Life, in Thy completeness held,
None can beyond Thy omnipresence stray;
Safe in Thy love, we live and sing alway
Alleluia! Alleluia!

O perfect Mind, reveal Thy likeness true,
That higher selfhood which we all must prove,
Joy and dominion, love reflecting Love,
Alleluia! Alleluia!

Thou, Soul, inspiring—give us vision clear,
Break earth-bound fetters, sweep away the veil,
Show the new heaven and earth that shall prevail.
Alleluia! Alleluia!

Grace for today, O Love divine,
Thee to obey and love alone;
Losing the mortal will in Thine,
Find we a joy before unknown.

Grace for today, Thou Love divine,
Famishing hearts and hopes to feed;
Blot out all fear, let Thy light shine
With tender warmth on all our need.

Grace for today, Thou Love divine,
Patient of heart his way to trace
Whose pure affections Thee define
In tender love and perfect grace.

Give me, O Lord, an understanding heart,
That I may learn to know myself in Thee,
To spurn the wrong and choose the better part
And thus from sinful bondage be set free.

Give me, O Lord, a meek and contrite heart,
That I may learn to quell all selfish pride,
Bowing before Thee, see Thee as Thou art
And ’neath Thy sheltering presence safely hide.

Give me, O Lord, a gentle, loving heart,
That I may learn to be more tender, kind,
And with Thy healing touch, each wound and smart
With Christly bands of Love and Truth to bind.

I cannot always trace the way
Where Thou, Almighty One, dost move;
But I can always, always say
That God is Love.

When mystery clouds my darkened path,
I conquer dread and doubts reprove,
In this my heart sweet comfort hath,
That God is Love.

Yes, God is Love: a thought like this
Can every gloomy thought remove,
And turn all tears, all woes, to bliss,
For God is Love.

O weary pilgrim, lift your head,
For joy cometh in the morning;
For God in His own Word hath said
That joy cometh in the morning.

REFRAIN
Joy cometh in the morning,
Joy cometh in the morning;
Weeping may endure for a night,
But joy cometh in the morning.

Our God shall wipe all tears away,
For joy cometh in the morning;
Sorrow and sighing flee away,
For joy cometh in the morning.

REFRAIN

In Love divine all earth-born fear and sorrow
Fade as the dark when dawn pours forth her light;
And understanding prayer is fully answered,
When trustingly we turn to God aright.

And as on wings of faith we soar and worship,
Held by God's love above the shadows dim,
Hushed in the grandeur of a heart's awakening,
Unfolds a joy unknown till found in Him.

Then in this radiant light of adoration,
We know that man beloved is in God's care,
Not wrapt in fear nor bowed with tired labor,
But satisfied, complete, divinely fair.

I walk with Love along the way,
And O, it is a holy day;
No more I suffer cruel fear,
I feel God's presence with me here;
The joy that none can take away
Is mine; I walk with Love today.

Who walks with Love along the way,
Shall talk with Love and Love obey;
God's healing truth is free to all,
Our Father answers every call;
'Tis He dispels the clouds of gray
That all may walk with Love today.

Come, walk with Love along the way,
Let childlike trust be yours today;
Uplift your thought, with courage go,
Give of your heart's rich overflow,
And peace shall crown your joy-filled day.
Come, walk with Love along the way.

O God, our Father-Mother, Love,
Purge Thou our hearts from sin,
That in Thy radiancy divine
We may with eyes undimmed define
Thy will, reality.

O God, our Father-Mother, Truth,
Send forth Thy light sublime,
That in its pure and cleansing rays
We may, with thought attuned to praise,
Behold reality.

O God, our Father-Mother, Life,
Reveal in us Thy might,
That henceforth we may live to Thee,
In all our ways reflecting Thee,
And know reality.

429

George W. Doane
Adapted

Thou art the Way: to thee alone
From sin and death we flee;
And he who would the Father seek,
Must seek Him, Lord, by thee.

Thou art the Truth: thy word alone
True wisdom doth impart;
Thou only canst unfold that Truth,
And purify the heart.

Thou art the Life: the rending tomb
Proclaims thy conquering arm;
And those who put their trust in thee
Nor death nor hell shall harm.

Thou art the Way, the Truth, the Life:
Grant us that Way to know,
That Truth to trust, that Life to learn,
Whose joys eternal flow.

First Lines

First lines of hymns by Mary Baker Eddy are printed in italics.

First Line No.

First Line No.

First Line No.

EDB0705005